# Butt and Ben

## A HIGHLAND BOYHOOD

# DONALD SUTHERLAND

BIRLINN

This edition published 2012 by
Birlinn Limited
West Newington House
10 Newington Road
Edinburgh EH9 1QS

www.birlinn.co.uk

First published in 1963 by
William Blackwood & Sons Limited

ISBN: 978 1 874744 428 3

British Library Cataloguing-in-Publication Data
A Catalogue record for this book is available from the British Library.

Typeset by Hewer Text UK Ltd, Edinburgh
Printed and bound by Clays Ltd, St Ives plc

IN MEMORIAM

NANCY BARTON
A Highland Lady
1871–1962

Ne Obliviscaris

# Contents

# Introduction

As someone who had the great good fortune to move into the Highlands over fifty years ago, I feel honoured and glad to write this introduction. Anything which extols the virtues of the Highlands and Argyll, and Oban in particular, gets my support. I am also glad to commend this book because it is entertaining and informative, going back as it does to the times before the First World War. And how much has changed since then. Donald Sutherland tells of meeting a former soldier whose means of attack was to sit on a horse with a lance and gallop forward until he was able to drive the lance into an enemy. Only fifty years later millions of people could be annihilated by just the press of a button from hundreds or even thousands of miles away.

Donald Sutherland obviously enjoys people, and in *Butt and Ben* brings many characters to life. He devotes a chapter to 'The Eccentrics' and later in the book tells of a ferryman who always wore a top hat. It was only after his sudden death when a policeman was carrying out the usual investigation that the true reason for this was discovered. Being puzzled by the weight of the hat, the policeman opened it up to discover that the upper part of it contained a small tin cistern filled with newly distilled whisky – the ferryman's way of defeating the Inland Revenue.

The distinctive and essential characteristics of the Highlander are brilliantly described. It is pointed out that we look at things slightly differently than our English neighbours and advice is given that if we 'wish to lead a pleasant and satisfactory life, you should pitch your tent where the tempo of life is slow'. A friend of Sutherland's from Shetland said to him one day, 'Up here we have time to live.' That doesn't mean that worthwhile things cannot be achieved in the Highlands. It is, in fact, quite the opposite. We learn also of the ability of 'the Highlander to look you in the eye with a grave face while, inwardly, he is shaking with laughter'. I have often been the victim of that myself, especially in my early days in Oban!

Donald Sutherland was the son of John (later Sir John) Sutherland who, with a Land Agent from Morvern called Hosack, founded the long-standing legal firm of Hosack & Sutherland in 1880. By chance it was that firm I joined when I came to Oban in 1960 and where I worked for nearly half a century before retirement, soon after which the name of the firm was changed to MacPhee & Partners. John Sutherland was the first full-time commissioner for the Forestry Commission, and after leaving Oban to work in Edinburgh he was knighted for his services.

With no specific connection, the Sutherland name cropped up again in the 1970s with the popular TV series *Sutherland's Law,* which dealt with the work of a Procurator Fiscal based in a fictional Highland town generally recognised as Oban. It certainly helped the tourist trade, and the Fiscal's role was brilliantly played by that great Scottish actor, Iain Cuthbertson.

Connections in the Highlands (as in Scotland as a whole) are not unusual and often noteworthy. For example, the house where Donald Sutherland was brought up and which is frequently featured in the book was Ardconnel House, which in 1946 was purchased by Bill Liddell, later a partner in Hosack & Sutherland. It is now owned by the Crerar family. Bill Crerar arrived in Oban almost at the same time as me and became a successful architect with commissions in different parts of the UK. He was noted also for his charitable giving, a tradition which is maintained now by his son, Paddy, of the Crerar Hotel Group. One of his recent donations was to the group which is now trying to revive the Oban cinema which has been defunct since 2010. It is therefore interesting to read in Donald Sutherland's book of the building of Oban's first cinema almost a hundred year ago.

Donald Sutherland captures well the nature and beauties of Argyll's countryside, and his description of landing his first salmon as a teenager has become a classic even for someone, like me, not interested in that particular sport. It was also the day that, although underage, Donald enjoyed his first malt, and that day was capped by a marvellous moonlit journey from the River Awe back to Oban in a carriage drawn by two horses. Of course, we can still enjoy such journeys, but I wonder if the view would be appreciated as much in a car. Among the sporting activities Sutherland describes are shooting parties. Not long after that the participants in those outings were shooting human beings rather than grouse. After the war he detected a slight change of attitude: 'Shooting for the pot, yes, occasionally. But never shooting for shooting's sake.'

Sutherland was in a position to know how things worked and how the system operated – the circles his family moved in were often those of the landed gentry who owned and controlled things. There are worthwhile comments about the respective contributions to the Highlands for good or bad of the Lords Strathcona and Leverhulme. Interestingly, a lot of the families of landowners mentioned in the book were still connected to Hosack & Sutherland when I joined the firm fifty years later but they didn't stay with the firm for very long after my arrival. Maybe they detected my views about taxing the landed gentry – a subject on which our author has some useful contemporary comments!

I was glad to see reference to Dr Robert MacKelvie who delivered our author into this world and later became his godfather. He points out that the doctor was 'considered art and part of the family life'. We have been lucky ourselves here in having many doctors who went well beyond the call of duty to help families at difficult times. Early on in my time here I got excellent advice from one of them: 'Don't try changing the Highlander because, as sure as damnit, they will end up changing you!'

When I arrived in Oban, Hosack & Sutherland were still administering a Charitable Fund known as The Dr MacKelvie Hospital Trust, set up for the West Highland Hospital in Oban. Problems later arose because of the centralised administration of the health service. It then became necessary for me to enter into a conspiracy with the local surgeon (I had better not name him!). When the time came for a distribution of funds the surgeon made application for funding a vital item of medical equipment needed by the local people, the cost of which, by apparent coincidence, was exactly the same as the amount to be distributed. There was also a separate MacKelvie Hospital, which lasted until the Oban General Hospital was completed in about 1995.

Donald Sutherland has a good recall of the cultural interests of those days and the dangers of Gaelic dying out were recognised. I am sure the author would have approved of the promotion of the language in the 1980s and 1990s by Argyll & Bute MP Ray Michie. She insisted on taking the oath in Gaelic when she went to the House of Lords, something which did not find favour with certain English Lords!

The spectacular views to be had from Ardconnel House are well depicted, the author concluding: 'There may be lovelier views than that but I have yet to see them.' And so say most of us!

Graeme Pagan
Oban
January 2012

# Foreword

WHATEVER is set down here is set down altogether from memory, and memory is a tricky jade. Anyhow, what follows is a picture of things remembered, or, to be even more precise, as they have grown in my recollection. I have no diaries or papers to consult.

It is very seldom that even highly trained witnesses, like good newspaper reporters, will give exactly similar accounts of the same event, as any news editor knows, and memory is even less reliable than sight. It also has the habit of dwelling upon what has been agreeable and passing over the disagreeable. Listen to the talk at any British Legion gathering if you want to know what I mean.

The past fifty years have been the most restless, the most violent and the most murderous in world history. All this book attempts is a record of the calm before the storm. If the storm has swept away much that was of ill repute – extremes of poverty, lack of opportunity, extremes of class consciousness and of insularity – it has also taken with it certain simple virtues: independence, self-reliance, courtesy and personal courage. All four, one likes to think, Highland virtues, and still more in evidence in the Highlands than south of the Highland Line.

In 1915 I spoke with a man who had couched his lance, sat down in the saddle, and galloped through rifle-fire to drive the lance head through the plastron of an Uhlan officer. That was a technique directly derived from Bannockburn and Agincourt. Forty years have put a weapon in the hands of man which slaughters indiscriminately by the hundreds of thousands. Two wars, a social revolution achieved without bloodshed, the passage of world leadership from our hands to inexpert, and possibly unwilling, fingers beyond the Atlantic; the growth of Communism, the menace of China, the third resurgence of German power encouraged and financed by those who nearly ruined themselves to break it . . . radio . . . television . . . penicillin . . . the atomic submarine . . . the sputniks. What a half-century! We are far, far more remote from our immediate ancestors than a Georgian farmer was from a yeoman of Edward III.

*Plus ça change* . . . The late Mr Bernard Shaw in his preface to 'Caesar and Cleopatra' poured scorn upon those who, in his time, regarded themselves as being more 'civilised' than the Romans. Techniques are not civilisation. There is still room in the world for the simple virtues, especially courage, and not that type of courage symbolised by sitting down in Trafalgar Square and other undesirable places.

In all this confusion and uncertainty, a reminder that peace, security and prosperity could, and did, exist in these islands may not come amiss.

# Argyllshire Boyhood

THE County of Argyll has always been different. A look at the map will explain why. To the west lie the Islands and the Atlantic. On the south and east the Firth of Clyde runs right up to Lochgoilhead, whence a stretch of mountain, bog and moor reaches to Rannoch and, westerly, to Kinlochleven. Inside those boundaries, reigning from his seat at Inveraray, the Mac Calein Mor, the Chief of Clan Campbell, was King. That the rest of the world knew their Chief as Duke, Marquess or Earl meant nothing to the Campbells. If the Mac Calein Mor condescended to become Lord Justice General or Master of the Royal Household in Scotland, good and well. If the King's Writ ran anywhere in Argyll it was by courtesy of Mac Calein Mor, and when he married the Queen's daughter, no Campbell doubted about who was honouring whom in such a marriage. But not all Argyllshiremen were Campbells. There were also Macdonalds, Macleans, Stewarts, MacDougalls and MacGregors who were not always in agreement with Inveraray except as regards interference from without. Constant fighting engenders lawlessness, and even today the men of Argyll have an instinct for the evasion of unpopular laws and give the Customs and Excise authorities a certain amount of trouble. During the last war, Glaswegians could motor into Argyll and return with unrationed eggs and legs of 'braxy' mutton. The incidence of suicide among Argyllshire's flocks was remarkable.

Fifty years ago my father lived at Oban, on the West Coast, where he was a man of considerable influence. He was not rich as the world then understood riches, nor was he poor. His practical common sense, his ability in public affairs and his essential humanity won him the respect of the agricultural community. His enjoyment of sport in every form (with one notable exception he was the finest shot with a twelve-bore gun I ever saw) won him a place of his own in the county. This must be explained here and now, otherwise it might seem improbable that his undistinguished son could have known the people who appear in these pages, or could have led the kind of life he did. Today it is only available to the very rich or to the few who still keep their ancestral acres.

In 1900, Argyllshire knew not telephones, motorcars or aeroplanes. There were no radios, cinemas or television sets. Some of these things may have existed elsewhere, but not in the county of Argyll. Person to person communication, when not oral, was by letter or telegram. Postcards were looked upon as vulgar. One travelled by steam locomotive, paddle-steamer and by sail. For short distances, behind, or on, a horse. When you dined away from home, you also spent the night, if not the week-end, with your host. Where you now spend a week-end, your visit would then have lasted a week. Visiting was very important. Spring, summer and autumn brought a constant round of visiting and visitors. My mother, a very social person by nature, spent at least three months of the year in other people's houses, and our own spare bedrooms were seldom empty from one year's end to the next.

The climax of all this visiting was reached in September when the Argyllshire Gathering took place. The Highland Games were attended by everyone who was anyone in the county and every laird and shooting tenant brought his own party. The Games were followed by two regattas, there were the Royal West Highland Yacht Club and the Corinthian Yacht Club, every room in every hotel was booked weeks in advance, there were the Gathering Ball and the Yacht Club Ball and for these a perfect frenzy of private entertainment. Thirty or forty yachts anchored in the bay. The *Mingaray*, Rudd of Ardnamurchan's 1000-ton beauty;

the Duke of Sutherland's *Sans Peur*; the Duchess of Bedford's *Sapphire*; the *Iolaire* (Gaelic for Eagle and pronounced Yewleragh) of Sir Donald Currie, the P. & O. Chairman; the Inverclydes' black yacht and dozens more. On regatta nights they were all illuminated and the fireworks were something worth seeing. Outside the bay, off the north end of the Island of Kerrera, half a dozen battleships of the Channel Squadron lay at anchor and contributed their own dinners, dances and searchlight displays. By day, their pinnaces and picket-boats threaded in and out of the yachts, their brass funnels glittering in the sunlight. The big racing yachts hoisted white sails and beat out of the bay to the starting-point off Maiden Island. Today such a show might be found at Monte Carlo, but nowhere else in Europe.

Then one morning the bay would be empty, the great grey warships would steam south down the Sound of Mull, the hotels were empty as the bay, our guests all went home and we settled down, like bears, to hibernate. Most of Oban's burgesses lived on the tourist trade for three seasons and their own fat for the fourth.

Our house stood above the town, some two hundred yards back from the edge of a steep cliff which screened the houses, huddled between the cliff's foot and the sea, from view. We looked west across the bay to the Island of Kerrera. Beyond Kerrera lay the Sound of Mull, with Mull itself, a great, greyish-purply mass dominated by Ben More, as a backcloth.

There may be lovelier views than that, but I have yet to see them. Fortunes of peace and war have taken me into four continents and ten times as many countries, but never have I seen such sunsets as when we watched the sun sink behind the Mull hills on a clear summer's evening. In the tropics your sun goes down with a blaze and a bang. The West Highland sun, characteristically, sinks slowly, pavilioned in a splendour of gold and green, of scarlet, violet and purple.

The house was set in fairly extensive 'policies' as we call 'grounds' in Scotland. There were several acres of larch and pine woods, a large garden at some distance from the house on a south slope with a tiny lochan below it. The lochan was the home of three fat trout, we knew them by name (Shadrach, Meshach and Abed-nego), who defied the skills of some of the world's best anglers as long as we lived there. Behind the house itself was a drying green (mother would have thought foul scorn to employ a laundry), dominated by a bogus peel tower which camouflaged a water-tank. Some previous owner must have been very tower-minded, because he built a second, this time a square tower, on to the south gable of the house. In it were three rooms, one above the other, but no stair of any kind; nor was there access from the house itself. You reached each room by ladder from the floor below. The bottom rooms were used for storage, but the top room was mine, my very own private domain. Once inside it, you pulled up the ladder after you. You were impregnable.

My room had three small windows. One looked across to Mull, one down the Sound of Kerrera and over the railway pier where David MacBrayne's paddle-steamers tied up, and one northwards to Dunollie Castle, the ruined and ivied keep of the MacDougall Chiefs, which guarded the narrow entrance to the bay. Given, as I was, an old stalker's spyglass, very little could happen in the neighbourhood without my knowing about it. School friends who came to stay during the holidays positively drooled with envy of my private Tower. And there were lots of distractions. Practising with dry fly on the lochan, very tricky and difficult owing to the trees and therefore very good for one; trying to get a rabbit for the pot with an airgun and, later on, learning to use a sixteen bore under strictest supervision . . . and there was golf.

Social strata were more clearly defined and more carefully preserved than they are today. Horizontally speaking, the top layer consisted of the County. One became County by owning an estate in Argyllshire or by having oneself born into a landowning family. Status within that class depended less on wealth than upon length of establishment.

Then came the professions. Lawyers: Oban boasted a Sheriff-Substitute's Court so there were lawyers galore. There was a magnificent collection of clergy, ranging from the Roman Catholic Bishop to a Baptist minister and passing through all degrees of Episcopalianism and Protestantism in between. Doctors we had, of course, and bankers. Bankers were for the most part local solicitors who became agents – there were no managers in those days – for one or other of the big Glasgow or Edinburgh banks. Also, as in most seaside towns, there were a few retired soldiers and sailors and their wives. Tradesfolk, who came next, were kept very firmly in their places, possibly because some of them could have bought up half the county without serious inconvenience. The lowest layer was composed of labouring men, their wives and 'the deserving poor'. The agricultural community were a law unto themselves. Their associations, outside their own kind, tended towards county more than anything else. Most of them were tenant farmers and crofters; very, very few farmed their own lands. The tenant's relation to his laird varied between the warm, close and contented . . . more often than not . . . to the cold, distant and quarrelsome. Ties of mutual interest and shared pleasures kept the outdoor people together.

But there was one factor in Argyllshire society not to be found elsewhere. I have said that Argyllshire was different. It cut vertically across all layers of society and its roots were deep in a distant and bloody past. You were either a Campbell or sib to the Campbells . . . or you were not.

Now the greatest man in the county was the Duke of Argyll. No one who was not himself a Campbell would think of denying it. Nearly all the Campbell lairds were vassals of Argyll. And his pre-eminence was sealed by his marriage to Princess Louise. And, as though that were not enough, he was followed in the Tables of Precedence by another Campbell, the Marquess of Breadalbane. Both magnates were Knights of the Garter, both owned great castles and huge tracts of moor, bog and mountain, both entertained royalty right royally; but to those who were not

Campbells . . . well . . . they were great men . . . but . . . could
one quite, altogether, trust any Campbell? There had been that
business at Glencoe and other affairs equally unsavoury. One met
Campbells, of course; how could one avoid it? One was polite to
Campbells at the Gatherings. One might dance with a Campbell
lass, and very lovely some of them were; one might take a dram
with a Campbell. As to that, Lord Breadalbane will always be
enshrined in my memory as the first man who ever asked me to
have a whisky and soda. Being only fifteen at the time and accompanied by my father, the offer had to be refused, but it raised my
schoolboy morale sky high even to be considered eligible for such
hospitality. Nevertheless one seldom asked Campbells to one's
house, and never asked them to stay any more than one visited
them. Memories are still long in the west. When the Duke's
brother, Lord Archibald, went to stalk in a forest which marched
with Glencoe, the Head Stalker, one Ian Macdonald, took charge
of him. Both men were sharing their sandwiches and a flask about
midday when Lord Archibald, the most genial and pleasant of
men, said jokingly:

'Well, Macdonald, it must be a change for you to take out a
Campbell. Not many of us up here, eh?'

'Oh, there are many Campbells hereabouts, my Lord. Many of
them there are.'

'Really?' – Lord Archibald sat up –'I wouldn't have expected
that.'

'If you cross over the Ben there,' Macdonald pointed, 'you
will be finding yourself in Inverlochy, and there are six hundred
Campbells there . . . in the kirkyard.'

At Inverlochy, Montrose inflicted the most shattering defeat
Clan Campbell ever suffered on the then Earl of Argyll in 1644.
The dead were buried in the churchyard. It is much to Lord
Archibald's credit that he told the story against himself. Memories
are long in the west.

As for Breadalbane, in 1901 a certain James McTavish of
Doune, a Breadalbane tenant, celebrated the superbity of the

Marquess in the following verses. They have not, to the best of my knowledge, appeared in print but have been passed from father to son in the county.★

> 'Frae Kenmore to Ben More
> The land is a' the Marquess's,
> The mossy howes,
> The heathery knowes
> And ilka[1] bonny park is his.
> The bearded goats,
> The toozie stots[2]
> And a' the braxy[3] carcases.
> Ilk[1] tinkler's tent,
> Ilk crofter's rent
> And ilka collie's bark is his.
> The muircock's[4] craw,
> The piper's blaw,
> The gillie's hard day's wark is his.
> Frae Ben More to Kenmore,
> The Warld is a' the Marquess's!'

[1] each, every; [2] shaggy, cattle; [3] meat from a beast that has died on the hill, *i.e.*, not slaughtered; [4] grouse.

*Sic transit gloria!* Today the House of Breadalbane possess no single acre of their ancestral lands. Taymouth Castle became an hotel, the Marquessate is extinct.

Father and mother occupied a position of their own. No man cared less about rank and position than father. Our family came from Inverness-shire and we never owned land in Argyll. The house was rented, and he rented also a neighbouring shoot at Soroba. But he was the senior male representative of a House that

★ Since writing this, I found, to my pleasure, the whole poem included in Ivor Brown's 'Chosen Words' (Penguin).

was granted arms by Robert the Bruce in 1309, was ennobled by Charles the Second, and lost its barony by attainder in 1715 for supporting Mar's ill-omened Rising. Mother, on the other hand, cared much about such things. There were three coronets in the branches of her family tree and, although she would never have said so, in her heart of hearts she was inclined to look upon the untitled as being indecently exposed. We were therefore outsiders in Argyll but acceptable outsiders. It helped a lot also that on my father's side we were descended from the Stewarts of Ardshiel, a property which at the time I am writing about had passed into Cameron hands. But it was Charles Stewart of Ardshiel, the Tutor of Appin, who commanded the Stewarts of Appin and Ardshiel all through the Forty-five, and for that reason the non- (I prefer non to anti) Campbells welcomed us the more warmly. But as a member of the county council, on which, naturally, Campbells predominated, father had much business with them and they did sometimes come to luncheon. So one learned at home that they did not all have tails concealed under their kilts and that they could be positively human . . . if Campbell.

My father-in-law, who was proud of his Campbell blood, thought that all Highland clans were equally bloodthirsty and barbarous, but the Campbells got away with more than the others because they were the first who bothered to learn reading and writing.

This peculiar clan consciousness was not by any means confined to county circles. Given local knowledge, you had only to read the accounts of Sheriff Court cases in the 'Oban Times' to understand that the greater part of pub brawling began by a word about a Campbell from a non-Campbell. I do not suppose this feeling could have lingered as long as it did if Argyllshire had not been so cut off from the rest of Scotland as it then was.

Churches and churchgoing played a big part in our lives. My mother's father was a clergyman of the Church of England. He took a living in the east of Scotland because he could pick and choose, having private means, and because the living was within easy distance of some of the best salmon fishing in Scotland. We therefore attended the Episcopal Church *in* Scotland. Note the 'in'. An Episcopal Church *of* Scotland was then unthinkable, and many good Presbyterians who regarded Rome as the Whore of Babylon still looked upon the Episcopalians as enthusiastic amateurs. An Episcopal Church of Scotland was a contradiction in terms. The Old Religion quite simply regarded us as heretics, which never prevented them from being the best company of all the clerics. Because father was gifted with hard common-sense and was more-over very generous with his services, he became a churchwarden and held that office until the Dean of the Diocese began to evince symptoms of megalomania and proposed to build a cathedral where no cathedral was desirable or even needed. Father resigned, a more pliable churchwarden was found, and the church plunged headlong into a morass of debt and worry, an orgy of begging and bazaars that, I have been told, continues even unto this day. The Dean's bitterness at father's defection was not sweetened when he was proved to be right and our two families ceased to know each other.

This was a severe blow to me. The Dean's youngest daughter and I had shared prams. She was a wonderful girl. She could poach trout, not in the culinary sense, with the best of us, she could ride anything with four legs and swim like a fish. She could recite Tennyson's 'Princess' at the drop of a hat . . . the hat was not dropped very often . . . she was handy with a bow and arrow and, best of all, she had a birthmark shaped like the island of Cyprus on her left leg. This she would display to friends free of all charge. Interested strangers had to pay threepence. As the threepences were always spent in Miss Mitchell's sweet shop and most generously shared, our separation was a blow. To us the ban seemed unreasonable. But children obeyed their parents in those days. After a few secret assignations in the woods of Dunollie Avenue it became too difficult and our friendship petered out.

Before this break there were always clergy about the house. When Diocesan Conferences took place, all four spare bedrooms were full, sometimes two curates to a bed. Once the Bishop stayed with us when the Dean's family were afflicted with measles. Mother enjoyed Bishops. Not so her father. Grandfather referred to them disrespectfully as 'those fat cats'. He owned a blue Persian called Peter who shared his sentiments. Peter, purring, would leap onto episcopal knees, deign to accept episcopal caresses and settle down, still purring like a kettle. Then, suddenly, all his claws went home through the black knee breeches and he would be shot off to sometimes unseemly objurgations. We firmly believed that grandfather had trained him to do it. At his own parsonage in Kincardineshire, grandmother had the strictest possible orders to serve discouraging meals whenever Bishops were about and a specially bad claret was kept in grandfather's otherwise admirable cellar, '*pour décourager les Evêques*'. Grandfather was a remarkable man of whom you will hear more later.

The break with the church did not put an end to our church-going. We went every Sunday as before, walking there and back. On Sundays the horses were rested. One wore Sunday best. It was a horrible, elaborate parody of everyday wear, which in summer consisted of a flannel shirt, open at the neck, an old kilt, a leather sporran, a sharp *skian dubh* when one wore stockings, and ancient brogues. In really hot weather the stockings were omitted and sand-shoes took the place of brogues. No Highland boy wears anything under his kilt. But Sunday best meant my 'best' kilt, a 'best' kilt jacket of green cloth with lozenge-shaped, crested, silver buttons, a silver-topped otter-skin sporran, Eton collar and tie, tartan stockings with a *skian dubh*, a special one which was blunt and had a cairngorm set in silver on the hilt, patent-leather shoes with buckles – and gloves. Yes . . . gloves. To make matters worse there was a Balmoral bonnet.

After church one walked along the esplanade. As all the churches and kirks 'skailed' at the same time, we met everybody we knew. The Balmoral had to come off at every meeting, and there is no way of taking the thing off without messing up your hair each time you do. It was forbidden to carry the thing, one had to take it off 'to show respect'.

On one of these detested occasions I was herded towards two old ladies who sat side by side on one of the public benches facing the sea. One of them wore widow's weeds. Mother pulled me aside.

'You are going to be presented to this old lady. If she holds out her hand, you must bow over it and kiss it.'

'Whaaat?'

'There's no time to argue. Just do what you are told.'

I looked towards father. No comfort there. We advanced. Father took off his hat and stood holding it. He and mother were talking something I recognised as French. Suddenly two great greeny-hazel eyes flashed at me. There was a smile and a jewelled hand was held out. I bent clumsily and did the awful thing. In front of everybody. Then mother made a funny little bob, father bowed and put on his hat and we moved away. When we were out of earshot, mother said:

'Now you can tell your friends that you have been presented to the Empress of the French.'

'But . . .'

'Well . . . what is it?'

'Father says that the French have a President.'

'They have now. But that lady was the last Empress. The Empress Eugénie. Don't forget.'

Well, you do not forget your first Imperial Majesty.

From a small boy's point of view one great objection to the social scheme of things was that it limited one's acquaintance in a neighbourhood where children of one's own age and status were few, too far between and far too female. After going to school that problem solved itself, because my friends came to stay with us in the holidays and I went to stay with them. But till then one was often lonely. Mother's law was as those of the Medes and the Persians. No fraternisation with children whose parents could not be invited to tea. Now tea was a reasonably eclectic kind of feast. But for my friends . . . definitely no.

That father secretly sympathised with me, I had proof. He once stumbled on us brewing a picnic tea over a fire of sticks, passed by and said nothing. 'We' were Lachie, the son of our most prominent local poacher. His prominence lay in the fact that everybody knew he lived by poaching, yet nobody had ever caught him. Lachie was almost as accomplished as his father, and taught me a lot that was useful later on, but neither he nor his father could by any stretch of imagination be considered as guests suitable for mother's tea-table. There were two caddies from the Golf Club who supplied me with lost balls, and Ian Black, a railway porter's son and the deadliest shot with a cattie (catapult) in the county. And as they couldn't come to tea with me, I had to take tea to them with the help and connivance of Mrs O'Callaghan the cook.

At this point there really ought to be a fanfare of trumpets. Mrs O'Callaghan deserves no less. She played a most important part in my young life. Whenever I hear the hymn with the line 'Let me to thy bosom fly', Mrs O'Callaghan's plump ghost is at my elbow.

Discipline at home was severe but never, or practically never, unjust. There certainly was no nonsense about the irreparable damage caused by physical chastisement to the psyche of the young. Endearments, nicknames and the like were frowned upon. Mother was mother, father was father. Never mum or mama or dad or daddy. Returning from prep school I once horribly ventured on 'pater' and 'mater'; after all, the other fellows called their parents pater and mater, but I was told clearly and firmly that small boys should not show off and both 'father' and 'mother' were good English words. When father was not father, he was sir, and to address either parent by a Christian name was quite unthinkable. Displays of emotion, especially tears, were discouraged as being 'unmanly'. So when the pony threw me into a bed of nettles or when I skinned my knees on the gravel and needed a bosom to weep on, Mrs O'Callaghan's starched prints absorbed my tears. Bless her! May she rest in peace! It was a wonderful bosom, ample, soft and filled with the milk of human kindness. None other, because the Mrs before her name was merely an official title. In those days all cooks were 'Mrs' regardless of their matrimonial status. She was also a teetotaller and more frequently pie-eyed than any teetotaller I knew before or since. This was not due to any lapses or infractions of the pledge she had signed. It was simply that Mrs O'Callaghan looked upon port as a teetotal beverage. When mother first became aware of her beliefs, she wanted to sack Mrs O'Callaghan. Father was instructed to check the contents of the cellar. Not so much as a half-bottle was missing. Then a surprising thing happened. Father broke an absolute rule of his lifetime and interfered in a purely domestic concern. Mrs O'Callaghan was to stay. And stay she did, for twenty-five years. She was a superb cook and honest as the day. Later it came out that she bought her own wine, at two shillings the bottle, from the grocer who supplied altar wine to the Roman Catholic Pro Cathedral. Mrs O'Callaghan was convinced that no evil could lurk in any liquid handled by the good priests. She could always be counted upon to rise to any occasion, and as she rose, the level of the wine in her bottle fell. The wine was always lukewarm because she kept it on a special shelf of her own behind the boiler. She had her favourites among our guests as among the family, and one of these was Colonel Sir Ian Malcolm of Poltalloch. He was a bearded, jovial man who never forgot to send his compliments to Mrs O'Callaghan after eating one of her meals. He had been a diplomat, was something of a gourmet, and his compliments were sincere. Once the level in the bottle fell so low that Mrs O'Callaghan burst into the dining-room, very red in the face and waving a pepper-pot. 'Ah, me lovely gigot's spoiled,' she cried, 'and me after forgettin' to pepper it to the Colonel's taste.' That time Poltalloch paid her his compliments in the kitchen and there were rumours that he had kissed her soundly.

For all her soft heart, she ruled her spotless kitchen with a rolling-pin of oak, and transgressors had been known to feel its weight. Her staff consisted of a tablemaid, two housemaids, a scullery maid and a boy. The tablemaid, Maggie MacInnes, was a handsome girl who came to us, practically unbroken, a wild filly from the Isle of Uist. After eight years with mother, she left us for Buckingham Palace where she served Queen Mary for eight more. During that time she married a sergeant of the Scots Guards who was killed in 1917. After the war she came back to my mother and was with her when she died in 1956. These two were the hard core of the indoor staff. Outside there was a gardener, a coachman-groom who turned into a chauffeur-valet as time marched on, and that prop of all Highland houses, the orraman who did the odd jobs, carpentered, painted, dug and mended. He, in our case, changed frequently, because father used to fill the job with some reprobate he hoped to reclaim, and Mrs O'Callaghan would keep her eagle eye on him and wage perpetual war.

By the standards of the time, ours was a very modest household. Menservants were uncommon in Scottish country houses. The butlers and footmen who arrived with shooting tenants were looked at askance by our folk who dubbed them 'he-housemaids', and they were seldom encountered except in houses where the master and mistress wintered in the south. Such people were seldom popular. The more time the laird and his family spent at home, the better they were liked. Absenteeism was resented. The stay-at-homes spent the winter among their own people, knew what they were up against and were quicker to appreciate difficulties and to help when help was needed. A laird who could come and see a leaking roof with his own eyes, and give immediate order for the necessary repair, was plainly preferable to an absentee who worked through a factor who, in turn, might have to obtain the permission, get estimates from two or three contractors, submit the lowest and so on, while the water continued to pour in.

In those days we still had language troubles. Not all the population could speak English. There were two stout women who came each Wednesday morning to deal with the week's laundry in an outhouse equipped with coppers, boilers, ironing-tables and the like. Neither of them had a word of English, only Gaelic. Maggie MacInnes, to whom English was a foreign tongue – she certainly thought in Gaelic – acted as interpreter. When she discovered that one of these women was teaching me to repeat Gaelic obscenities after her, there was a tremendous Gaelic hullabaloo in the back-yard, the reason for which was not revealed till years later. I was never to learn more than a few phrases of Gaelic. My father spoke a little but understood quite a lot. Among farmers and crofters, however, the Gaelic was widely spoken and you would hear little else at cattle or sheep sales or in the pubs afterwards. But in fifty years it has practically died out, in spite of valiant but somewhat precious efforts to keep it alive. On the mainland of Scotland today you will hardly ever hear Gaelic spoken, and anyone who has wrestled with Gaelic orthography will understand why. There is no Gaelic literature worth speaking about, and a language without literature is a language without roots.

Lastly a word about dress. We wore the kilt. Not 'kilts' and never 'the kilts'. It is an excellent garment. It is hygienic, as nearly everlasting as any woollen garment can be, warm in winter and cool in summer. It gives more freedom of movement than any other and, properly worn, is handsomer than any other provided the wearer has decent legs. Those of us entitled to do so wore our clan tartans, and you could tell a Campbell afar off by his green kilt. Today, tartans are mostly woven in the Lowlands where shrewd men of business work at selling more and more of their product. They have gone to town on the sales of tartan. They have invented scores of tartans never heard of twenty years ago. They have added septs to clans and septs to septs till they are in the happy position of being able to find a tartan for almost anyone at all. Rosenberg? That is easy. Montrose, that's Graham, isn't it? And Mrs Rosenberg happily flaunts a Graham tartan skirt. Be you Vanderbilt, Habsburg, Valois or Glucksberg, the Edinburgh shops will kit you out with a clan tartan of some sort. If your sister-in-law's cousin married a Maclean, why, Maclean's your tartan . . . if you believe the vendor. English folk have abandoned even that pretence. They wear tartan 'as a compliment to the Scotch'. One in Perth wore the Black Watch tartan 'in honour of the Regiment' till certain privates of that honourable Regiment tore it off him in a pub and sent him home in his shirt-tails.

But anyone can wear the kilt who wants to. Just forget about tartan and choose a tweed. A tweed kilt looks very handsome. It was the normal wear of English shooting tenants at the time I am writing about. It you want to be exclusive, have your own tweed specially designed for you and give lengths to your friends. Both King George V and King George VI so honoured their close companions on the moor and the hill.

But no tartan, please. We Highlanders look on this matter with a jaundiced eye. The tartan is a Highland dress and should be worn by Highlanders. Left-handed 'compliments' are not appreciated. The tartan is the clansman's robe of honour. Although in Scotland a man may be imprisoned for wrongfully using the coat of arms of another, there is no protection for the tartan, the last really practical manifestation of heraldry in the world today. It is no crime to wear another's tartan, but, to the Highlander's mind, which he will always be too polite to express, to do so is in the worst taste imaginable.

# The First American

FATHER was away from home. Because the right of chastising me physically was vested solely in his hands, when he was not at home I was forever subject to threats. 'When your father comes back I shall tell him about this.' And because these threats were never carried out I took them at their true value and paid no attention whatsoever. It is not a wise policy to turn one's father into a bogey man, especially when he is nothing of the kind. There was another thing that sometimes saved my hide. When justice was done upon my person, Mrs O'Callaghan would go pale and wild; worse still, her cooking deteriorated appreciably. As the sheer crassness of adults had just deprived me of the only congenial female society in the neighbourhood, I was feeling aggrieved by what John Knox so aptly described as the 'monstrous regiment of women'. In such crises one could only retreat to the Tower.

Having scrambled up the ladder and hauled it after me, I dropped the trap-door and found the spyglass. It was a breathlessly still, hot, August morning without a cloud in the sky. The bay was a sheet of sapphire. The *Fusilier*, one of David MacBrayne's fleet of paddle-steamers, was taking on passengers for Tobermory at the railway pier, and I could see Captain MacInnes, our Maggie's cousin, leaning over the port wing of the bridge and giving his laconic orders. Yachts were dotted about the bay. *Morag, Sapphire, Daphne*, the Clarks' *Christine* from Ulva and lots of others. I crossed to the north window. There was nothing there either . . . then I spotted it. A bowsprit coming into view from Loch Linnhe, just sliding round the cliff below Dunollie

Castle. Then a figurehead, a gold eagle . . . this was something new. Slowly and majestically a great yacht glided into the bay. She was black, with three masts like Lord Brassey's *Sunbeam*, but larger, and unlike the *Sunbeam* she was square-rigged. There was no breath of breeze to stir the folds of the ensign at her stern. She was coming in under power from her auxiliary engine. I could just make out a slim cream funnel aft. Her burgee hung as limp as the ensign. She was a whopper . . . almost as big as the *Mingaray*.

Up trap-door, down ladder, pound round to the front door.

'Maggie . . . where's mother?'

'In the garden.'

'Tell her I've gone down to the bay . . . there's a new yacht come in.'

'Very well, Master Donald. Mind you're not late for your lunch now!'

Usually when I wanted to dash off to town there were messages. Notes were written to the butcher or to the grocer or one was impounded to call in at some house or other. Remember, no telephones, and there were time-wasting delays while the notes were written. But not today.

Fifteen minutes later Angus MacLucas, who hired boats, had fixed me up with a light dinghy, a pair of sculls and a suitable admonition. 'Don't you pe chumping apout in the poat now, Master Donald!' Father ran an account with Angus and I could have an hour's boating a day whenever I liked during the season. I dropped one oar blade down through crystal water to the shingle below and shoved off.

We had no yacht of our own. Father was once very fond of sailing and owned a yawl in which he had several racing successes. The summer before I was born, he arranged with two friends to sail across to Lismore for an evening's trout-fishing in Loch Kilcheran. He was delayed that afternoon by some unexpected business and sent them word to take the yawl and go without him. They were both experienced sailors of small boats. None the less, on the return journey they were caught in a sudden squall off the Seal Islands, capsized and were both drowned. After which father sold the yawl and never sailed again.

To row round Oban Bay was always a pleasant ploy in any weather. I had lots of friends in lots of yachts: owners, skippers, engineers and crew. Many of them were West Highlanders themselves: engineers invariably came from the Clyde. They were kindly men, ready to pass the time of day with a red-headed lad in a dinghy and answer his questions, sometimes to pass down a slice of cake or a biscuit from the galley. But not today. The new black yacht was my target. She had anchored right in the middle of the bay. As I came closer the ensign was recognisable as the Stars and Stripes, and the name *Niagara* was carved in the scroll-work behind her eagle figurehead. The companionway had been lowered and a light, four-oared gig made fast to it. A look at the davits told me that a launch had gone ashore. A man in a Panama hat, with a cigar in his mouth, leaned on the taffrail, looking at Oban. I shipped my oars and drifted past.

'Hey . . . girlie!'

The hail was repeated twice or thrice. I looked round . . . there was no female within hailing distance. Was it possible? The man took the cigar from his mouth and pointed it straight at me . . . at *me*.

'Did you mean me, sir?'

'Sure, sure.'

I went hot all over. Me . . . girlie!

'I'm not a girl.'

'Then whaddaya wearin' skirts for? American boys wear pants.'

'In Scotland we wear the kilt!'

I got the oars out and tried to make a dignified getaway. Perhaps he recognised the magnitude of the insult he had offered. Anyway he chuckled and tossed his cigar into the water. Then he said, 'Guess I made a mistake, son. Maybe I'll know better next time. Never been in these parts before. Care to come aboard?'

Care to come aboard! I'd have given my eye-teeth to come aboard. The insult was forgotten in a flash.

'Yes, thank you very much. If it's all right?'

'Waal . . . I asked you, didn't I?'

'Yes, sir.'

'Then it sure is all right. Make fast 'longside the companion-way . . . and don't scratch my paint.'

What sort of a lubber did he think I was? Scratch his paint! Torn between wounded *amour propre* and curiosity, I got on deck.

*Niagara* was a beauty, a very proud beauty indeed, and it only needed a glance to see that she was given the care she deserved. The teak decks were as spotless as those of a battleship, the brass glittered in the hot sun, each rope was immaculately coiled down . . . as smart as the Royal Navy, and anyone knew there wasn't anything smarter than that. The owner, at least I took him to be that, turned me over to a young sailor. 'Show him anything he wants.'

He did. Everything. He even let me climb the ratlines, with due precautions, to a crow's-nesty kind of platform two-thirds of the way up the foremast. He showed me the engine-room, the crew's quarters, which were better than some of the offi-cers' cabins in other yachts, the shining galley with, wonder of wonders, a shiny *black* cook presiding, the owner's stateroom with its wide double bed and brocade bedspread and gold-backed hairbrushes (father's were only silver), the three guest staterooms, each more luxurious than the last and each a differ-ent colour, but all empty. And the bath, a marble bath on board ship! Then to the saloon, where he handed me over to the owner, saluted and slipped away before I could thank him. The saloon was panelled in light-coloured woods, with a sham fireplace at the after end between the doors which led to the staterooms. Over the fireplace, let into the panelling, was a great oil-painting, something I had never seen in a ship before. The owner was having a drink. He looked at me and decided that whisky was not yet for me, then he had an inspiration.

'Say, son . . . what about a dish of ice-cream?'

Ice-cream! In those days ice-cream was *something*. If one tasted ice-cream four times a year, that was a bumper year. Ice-cream was a treat of the first order. Of course it was made from fruit juice and real cream, not compounded from chemical flavourings and soya flour or whatever goes into the horrible synthesis sold as ice-cream today. Almost the only party of the whole year at which one could count on ice-cream was the grand children's party given before Christmas by Mrs MacDougall of MacDougall, the Chief's wife, at Dunollie House. But even her eagerly anticipated strawberry and vanilla paled into insignificance beside the gorgeous confection brought in by the steward. It was something like an Italian *cassata*, with fruits, nuts, glacé cherries, whipped cream and praline wafers. Also there was more than usual, much more than usual.

'Go ahead,' said my host, with a wave of his cigar. 'Lots more where that came from.'

More! The spirit was willing enough, but the storage capacity was limited. As I was half-way through this ambrosial dish my host nodded at the painting.

'Know anything about Old Masters, son?'

'No, sir.'

'Guess maybe you're a mite young for that. See that picture?'

It was the portrait of some very splendid personage with a brocade doublet, a ruff, a pointed beard and great dark eyes. He wore a jewelled chain round his shoulders and one hand rested on his sword-hilt. He was just my idea of a Spanish Don. I had been reading Mr W. G. Henty on the Spanish Armada.

'He looks like a Spaniard,' I said tentatively.

'Plumb in the bull's eye! He was a Don. And so was the painter. Velasquez was his name. Ever hear of him?'

'No, sir.'

'Guess you will some day. Would you believe me if I told you that the picture's worth more than *Niagara* and everyone aboard her, except me? . . . No, I guess you wouldn't. But it's true just the same. More ice-cream, son?'

I just couldn't. I finished what I had left and we went on deck together.

'Be about tomorrow, son?'

Tomorrow was full of dull chores, none of which could be escaped, and none of them could possibly lead up to ice-cream. I shook my head.

'Well' – he dragged out the word till it sounded like 'Waaaaal' – 'maybe the day after. Waiting here for a cable from America. Anyhow, if we're still here, come aboard.' He turned to a sailor beside us. 'Quartermaster, if this boy' – there was a slight emphasis on the 'boy', perhaps it was a form of apology – 'if this boy wants to come aboard any time, that's fine. And if I'm not around, tell the stoo'ard to give him ice-cream. He likes it.'

We shook hands.

'Thank you very much, sir. I've had a wonderful time.'

A wonderful morning for any boy and not a female in sight. As I rowed for the shore the station clock struck one. As the sound rolled over the water it was instantly apparent that there would be a price to pay for all this. Half an hour late for luncheon was a serious crime.

The penalty decreed was two hours' work in the garden. No excuses were asked for. I had, of course, just been mooning about the bay without a thought for anything but my selfish pleasure.

Mother, whose green fingers were legendary, she even had rhododendrons named after her, was incapable of understanding how anyone could really hate gardening. Normally it probably wouldn't have been too bad, but just at the moment John MacKechnie the gardener and I were not on very good terms. There had been an incident. Mixed up in it were my new Gem airgun, a B.B. pellet and John's brown-corduroyed behind. It was bad luck for me that just at the very moment when John leaped into the air like a salmon, using powerful words in Gaelic, father should happen to be standing at the library windows. But that's how it was. Father made straight for my hide in the branches of a Douglas fir, had me out of it, confiscated the gun and went into action; very, very painful action for . . . So there would be no interludes among the raspberry-canes or the gooseberry-bushes. Just hard work. And carting stones, in a wheelbarrow, for a rockery in a blazing August afternoon is hard work for anybody.

Parenthetically and in retrospect, that form of punishment, momentarily effective and well deserved as it was, had the result of killing my interest in gardens and gardening stone dead for years to come. Forty of them were to pass before a garden became the laborious delight it is today, and so forty years of potential knowledge have been lost for ever.

Sentence served, I went back to the house, only to be caught in the hall and sent upstairs to wash and brush my hair – not that brushing ever did any good to the copper wire I grew in those days. Then down to the drawing-room. It was mother's 'at home' afternoon, and in those days it was held that taking round cakes and scones, carrying cups to be refilled and the like had a civilising influence on the young. It was part of one's normal training. The cocktail brawl had not then been invented and tea was a social ritual of importance. In a corner of the drawing-room mother sat ensconced behind a silver tea-tray with silver teapot, cream-jug, kettle and other necessities. At her side was a cakestand of three tiers, and more silver vessels filled with hot buttered toast and scones stood before the fireplace on a low table.

Round her were disposed four or five ladies, their veils pushed up to free their jaws for champing, gloves in their laps and scandal on their lips. During the handing-round process I suffered the usual remarks about my growth, my hair (why do red-headed boys automatically become figures of fun?), and hopes were expressed that I had been a good boy lately. What a hope! If any of these excellent and kind women had been able to read my thoughts they would have been appalled by the venom and animosity their well-intentioned remarks had engendered in one so young. It was not until they began to discuss the *Niagara* that I really bothered to listen. She was, it appeared, a nine hours' wonder.

'Such a *big* black yacht. American they say . . . and what is so surprising, my husband says nobody has called at the Yacht Club.'

It was the custom for visiting yachtsmen to pay a courtesy call at the Royal Highland Yacht Club on the esplanade. Thereafter they were usually made free of its amenities.

'What?' said another. 'No call? How very peculiar!'

'Americans,' stated another, 'have no *savoir faire*.'

'I do know,' said the first, 'that nobody has gone aboard, and only one person from the yacht came ashore.'

'Most unusual,' brooded the second lady. Then she brightened up and anticipated Mr Norman Douglas and his 'South Wind'. 'Perhaps it's a millionaire with *several* chorus girls on board and he *daren't* let them be seen ashore!'

This delicious speculation stirred them up like bees whose bike has been poked with a stick. They made me sick. It was time to stand up for the dispenser of ice-cream. As if any sane person would take women on a yacht unless they had to!

'As a matter of fact,' I said, 'there are no ladies on the *Niagara*.'

'And how do you know that?' asked mother.

'Because I spent the morning on board her.'

It was the most sensational statement of my short life. All the hats immediately swivelled round and concentrated on me.

'How clever of you, Donald.'

'How did you manage it?'

'And who *is* the owner?'

And other female foolishnesses. Mother was not impressed. Her expression, which I knew very well, was one of extreme scepticism.

'You must remember, Mrs MacLachlan,' she said, 'that Donald's a very imaginative boy. I shouldn't be surprised if he hasn't imagined the whole thing.'

The emphasis on the word 'imagined' meant to me 'for "imagined" read "made up". Be careful!' Well, that touched me off. It all came pouring out. The whole history of my morning's adventures. Never before had I disposed of so appreciative an audience. At last I came to the Velasquez. Then there was silence. Mother still looked sceptical. She had reason for her doubts. Had I not once given her a vivid account of a meeting with real pirates in a cave near Ganavan (that came from finding the libretto of 'The Pirates of Penzance' in the music-stand)?

'Donald,' said mother, 'often amuses his little friends by making up stories for them.'

At this point Miss Janet took a hand in the conversation. To be precise, she took two. Miss Janet was a clever, good-looking girl in her late twenties who had the misfortune to be deaf and dumb. She was not merely 'artistic', she was a creative artist in her own right whose watercolours fetched good prices in London and whose wood-carvings brought Paris dealers all the way to Oban. Miss Janet was our oracle in all matters concerning the arts. She was my very good friend, but this time she was on the wrong side. It said a great deal for her charm and character that practically everyone in the neighbourhood learned to talk on their fingers in order to be able to communicate with Miss Janet. She could lip-read her friends with complete accuracy.

Miss Janet explained with flickering fingers that Velasquez portraits were very, very valuable indeed, and also that salt sea air was held to be very bad for oil-paintings. She didn't think that any owner of a genuine Velasquez portrait would be so rash as to take it to sea in a yacht however luxurious. Perhaps, she suggested, the owner had had it copied and carried the copy about with him.

Then mother shot a question at me.

'What was his name? Your friend on the yacht?'

Now he had never asked for mine and it just never occurred to me that I should ask for his. I shook my head and mother made up her mind.

'You've been romancing again. I don't believe a word of it.' And then she changed the subject.

Now if there is anything more infuriating than being disbelieved when you have told a flat lie, it is being disbelieved when you have told the truth, the whole truth and nothing but the truth. That night at bedtime there was a lecture about confusing what really happened with what you thought had happened, and about how wicked it was deliberately to mislead people in order to attract attention to yourself.

'At first,' said mother, 'I thought you were telling the truth, but when you made up that taradiddle about the portrait, I knew you were inventing and I felt very ashamed of you.'

Attract attention! And when I asked for nothing, nothing more than to get out of that henhouse! It just wasn't fair. I stuck my nose in my pillow and sulked. I wanted to leave mother out of my prayers that night and I almost did. I was furious.

Next morning there was no *Niagara* in the bay. The second dish of ice-cream had melted over the horizon and I was never to set eyes on the yacht again. Father came back from London that evening. He brought me a new kind of golf-ball called the Haskell which was supposed to go farther than the gutty Silvertown, and cost two whole shillings. As we three, father, mother and I, were walking in the garden after dinner, father said, 'Oh, I hear you had the American yacht in the bay. *Niagara*. I wish I'd been here to see her. Stirling Maxwell tells me that she sailed across from New York without using her engines. Belongs to a millionaire, Railways, I think, called Jay Gould. Maxwell said he hung a Velasquez in the saloon. Portrait of some Spanish count. Why? What are you laughing at?'

For mother began to laugh and laugh and laugh. Then she caught at my hand. 'You men,' she said. 'You always stick together, don't you?'

# The First Colonel

ALMOST every adult male over forty years of age has had some experience of colonels. As a race, if you can so describe them, colonels run to extremes. Like the little girl in the nursery rhyme: 'when they are good, they are very, very good, but when they are bad they are horrid'. In England today we suffer a plethora of colonels. Two fine examples at opposite ends of the scale flourish not far from where I am now writing. One was a civilian, a professional man, who got his rank for the exercise of his profession in war-time. The other spent his life in a guards battalion, rose to command it and collected a CB, a DSO and an MC with a Bar on the way. He may be described with complete accuracy, as service members of the House of Commons are described, an honourable and gallant gentleman. But to the man in the street, both are colonels. To appreciate the difference within the distinction, personal acquaintance is necessary.

That retired professional soldiers should use their rank in civil life is only right and proper. But among the amateurs this insistence on bygone glory seems to go hand in hand with failure or disappointment in civilian life. The multiplicity of such men cheapens the title for those who have honourably earned it the hard way. Perhaps the amateurs hope that those who know them to have been officers may be deluded into the assumption that they are also gentlemen.

Like every other amateur soldier, I have admired colonels, despised colonels, worked for and with colonels, lampooned colonels, sweated for colonels, cursed colonels and feared colonels. But the only colonel I ever loved was my very first colonel, Colonel James MacLeod. Colonel Jimmy is now in Paradise, for if any member of the human race ever reached that destination, Jimmy did.

Everybody knew him as Jimmy. Just Jimmy and forget the colonel, as he would implore his friends. He was a cadet of the Raasay Macleods and had spent the greater part of his life in India. There he was famous from Madras to Simla, from Calcutta to Bombay as a mighty horseman before the Lord. His regiment, and I believe he had a hand in the founding of it, was the Behar Light Horse. He was a confirmed bachelor, not rich, and content to live on the Corran esplanade at Oban, where his landlady, once she had recovered from the initial shocks produced by Jimmy's language and appearance, worshipped him and cherished him as only a good Scots landlady can.

He must have been the physiognomist's despair, for never was any man's nature less mirrored in his appearance. He was short and bandy-legged. At some time or other he must have broken nearly every bone in his body. His nose had suffered twice and had been pushed slightly out of the straight. His face was that of a benevolent Bardolph, with dark eyes set deep in a flaming fiery furnace of a face with a great white moustache stained brown by nicotine and burned ragged by the innumerable cigarettes he incessantly smoked. In spite of his complexion, Jimmy, even in his Indian prime, was a strict teetotaller. Because he himself was slightly deaf he did not converse so much as roar at you, and he had the disconcerting habit of speaking his thoughts out aloud without being aware of it. He swore imperially in several languages. When we were in mixed company I would hope against hope that Jimmy would do his cussing in Urdu or Tamil rather than in English, not because his language ever embarrassed me, but because it would have been intolerable that anyone who didn't know him should mistake him for the boor he most certainly was not.

The living-room in his lodgings was more like the butler's pantry of some stately home than anything else. Sideboards, the tops of bookcases, almost any flat surfaces in the room were crowded with cups, shields, vases, bowls, salvers of silver, salvers of silver gilt, each contributing its own quota to the legend of Jimmy, the best amateur jockey in all India. His landlady kept them immaculate, and if you walked along the esplanade of an evening you could see the glitter of gold and silver through the open windows. He was never burgled. If he had been, the burglar, if caught, would have been torn to pieces.

In Oban he was far the most kenspeckle figure in the whole town. Any summer morning, and on most winter ones too, you could see Jimmy walking – waddling sounds too unkind – through the town towards the golf-course. He wore a black-and-yellow striped blazer – the Macleod colours – brown tweed knickerbockers, Macleod tartan stockings with white spats on top of canvas rubber-soled shoes – his feet gave him trouble and leather hurt them – and a tartan tie. In summer this magnificence was crowned by a sola topi, in winter by a 'twa-snooted bunnet'; that is a deerstalker without ear-flaps. The pockets of his blazer bulged with a pound bag of mixed, boiled sweets on one side and a 'fifty' tin of his favourite cigarettes on the other. Every child in the town knew that he or she had only to go up and say, 'Guid day tae ye, Currnel', to be instantly rewarded with a peppermint ball or some such confection. Female children, however snotty, were saluted by a sweep of the topi which would have done honour to a duchess. Naturally, Jimmy's progress through the town was apt to be slow, and he seldom showed up on the first tee punctually.

He took up golf at the age of seventy with all the enthusiasm he had once devoted to polo, and played it as only he could play it, in a style which no one else in the world could or would be advised to imitate. He never brought the club-head past his shoulder. He flicked it round in a circle in front of him. However improbable it sounds, he could hit the ball fairly straight and sometimes broke the hundred. Those were red-letter days. Every good shot was followed by a roar of 'Whatteryethinknofthat!' If the ball was disobedient he encouraged it with shouts of 'Straight on, ye hoor, straight on!'

The last green lay below the club verandah. I've seen Jimmy literally dancing, putter in hand, as the ball rolled towards the hole, and roaring, 'Ye hoorish bitch, ye . . . go down, down or damn yer bloody eyes to hell.' He would walk through the assembled members and their wives, partaking genteelly of tea and scones, stop to look at a good-looking girl (Jimmy always had an eye for such), mutter audibly, 'Hah . . . collar of Venus . . . good between the sheets that one,' and stump on into the smoking-room without any idea of the blushes and confusion spread in his wake. It was just as well, for nothing would have troubled his gentle spirit more than the thought that he had offended any young woman.

Soon after Jimmy settled in Oban, my father's mother came to live with us permanently. Grandmother was crippled by acute arthritis. She had to be lifted from her bed like a child, put into a wheel-chair and pushed down the passage to her sitting-room, which overlooked the bay. There she held court. The old lady suffered a great deal of pain with the very minimum of complaint. She read very little, preferring the spoken to the written word and the society of human beings to any other diversion. Both father and mother were busy and active people with all kinds of friends and interests. I, like any ten-year-old, preferred to be outdoors rather than inside; so, inevitably, grandmother was alone for much of the day. With the thoughtless selfishness of young folk I sometimes even grudged to her the statutory hour a day I was ordered to spend with her. Our guests always called in to see her. Really kind people like Miss Janet made a point of going whenever they could, but grandmother's poor hands were too stiff for finger talk and she only wrote with great difficulty. She was also shrewdly aware that some of her visitors came in hope of currying favour with father and mother rather than for her own sake.

One day, after golf, I brought Jimmy back to the house for tea. It so happened that my mother was out, and Maggie suggested that we should have tea with grandmother in her sitting-room.

Just after the necessary introductions had been performed, I was called away about something or other and therefore cannot report on this first meeting of opposites. But its success was very soon apparent.

Grandmother could not have been described as a vain person, but she was extremely fastidious and very particular about what she wore. Like most old ladies of that era, inside the house she was always crowned with a small cap of lace and ribbons. Every year in the first week of December, grandmother's new lace cap arrived in a little round box from an address in the Rue St Honoré, Paris. The secret of the box was revealed at our Christmas dinner. Now, you could usually surmise the standing of any guest in grandmother's estimation by the cap she chose to wear during their reception. This year's cap was for close friends, last year's for pleasant acquaintances, and so on down to caps five or six years old for those who had little or no place in her esteem.

It was not long before she suggested that I might bring the colonel again, and when he came grandmother had on her very newest cap.

They were an odd couple. Grandmother, slight, all pink, white and silver in a black satin dress; Jimmy, solid, all the colours of the rainbow, sitting up straight in his chair (grandmother had that effect upon people), hands on his knees and his ring flashing in the firelight. He always wore a magnificent sapphire, big as a hazel-nut, set in diamonds, the gift of a maharaja whose horse he had steered to victory, and somehow or other on him it was not incongruous. It suited his personality. I once asked why he wore it. Jimmy winked portentously. 'Woman bait, me boy!'

Grandmother conducted the conversation in her clear, low-pitched voice which had just a touch of Highland cadence in it. Jimmy at first tried to emulate Bottom and roar gently as any sucking dove . . . till he grew excited . . . but he never swore in her presence.

He treated her with a deliberate, formal gallantry, roaring his old-fashioned compliments on her appearance, her health, or on

31

whatever she happened to be wearing, and somehow or other managed to create the illusion that she was an eligible débutante and he the gallant young officer of forty years ago. She adored it and he made her happy. As their friendship progressed, Jimmy used to call on her three or four times a week. Each call meant a stiff climb of at least two miles for his short, old legs. He never came empty handed. If it wasn't a bunch of flowers, it was a pot of preserved ginger, or a box of chocolates, or an illustrated magazine (grandmother liked to look at pictures), or a china cottage (she collected them). Always it was some trifle to bear witness to his constant thoughtfulness and devotion. Small wonder he became the light of her life, the chief subject of her conversation, and when he was not actually with her, she counted the hours till his next visit.

His patience and understanding as her end drew near and her mind became confused was little short of angelic.

Jimmy became so much *ami de la maison* that he had the privilege of walking straight into the house without ringing the bell, and no one else was allowed to do that. Like Poltalloch he, too, won Mrs O'Callaghan's heart, and whenever he lunched with us Mrs O'Callaghan had a curry fit 'to take the roof offn yer mouth' specially for him.

As grandmother grew progressively worse, Jimmy's visits became more and more frequent. It was 'more convenient' for him to walk up the hill with me after golf than take the cab that usually came to drive him back from the course to his rooms. Or he was pining for a cup of really good tea, he said; something, apparently, not to be found anywhere outside grandmother's sitting-room. Any pretext served to conceal the fact that he would do anything in his power to lighten the sufferings of a fellow being.

It seldom occurred to Jimmy that other men's standards might be less high than his own. He was once drawn in a golf competition against a certain bailie of the town, a man quite notorious for his mean-minded suspiciousness. After Jimmy had lost by the usual seven down and six, he was deep in the dumps and quite unlike his usual self. As we walked home together he suddenly stopped by the lochan.

'Hah . . . d'ye know, Donald, that bloody feller thought I was goin' to cheat him. Sneakin' up behind and countin' my strokes in the bunker . . . whaddoes he think I am?' Jimmy exploded in a shower of '*Soor ka butchas*', '*Soor ka Meranis*', '*Buddawa nis*', 'two-arsed bastards' and 'cheese-mongerin' whoresons'. Then he suddenly cheered up. 'Feller's only a bloody hairdresser,' he said more reasonably. 'Don't know any better I s'pose.' He himself was so much the soul of honesty that it genuinely shocked him to find that others might so much as suspect him capable of petty cheating.

Mother was once approached by a woman who suggested to her that Jimmy's language could not be good for my tender ears. Luckily, by that time, mother had come to appreciate Jimmy at something like his true worth. I didn't know what she said, but the lady in question never came near us again. As a matter of fact, Jimmy's cussing added to my status at school. Little pitchers have good memories as well as long ears. I could remember phonetically what he said and awed my contemporaries at second-hand with Jimmy's vocabulary.

If some time elapsed between my making Jimmy's acquaintance and his presentation to grandmother, there was a reason for it. She hated tobacco smoke. Not even father was allowed to smoke in her sitting-room. In her youth smoking was regarded as a male vice permissible only in smoking-rooms or, better still, in the great outdoors. It was a prejudice shared by the greatest in the land. A guest at Balmoral casually mentioned at breakfast that he had enjoyed a cigar before going to bed. 'You did? But how?' asked envious courtiers. 'Pushed aside the fender, dropped a cushion in the fireplace, lay down, lit up and smoked up the chimney,' replied the ingenious guest. He was a peer of the realm and a Cabinet Minister. Grandmother was no less adamant than the Dear Queen herself. She always talked about 'nasty tobacco', and when father smoked on the lawn outside her window he was requested by special messenger – me – to do it somewhere else, and meekly obeyed. Jimmy, on the other hand, must have smoked between seventy-five and a hundred cigarettes every day of his life, and was not really at his ease unless a cigarette was burning holes in his moustache. I just didn't believe he could last an hour without one. How grandmother discovered his craving I never knew, but one day she said, 'Colonel Jimmy.'

'Yas, ma'am.'

'I want you to do me a favour.'

'Hah . . . an honour, ma'am. You only have to mention it and you may consider it done.'

Jimmy was galloping away on his high horse.

'I would like you,' said grandmother, 'to indulge yourself with a cigarette.'

I just couldn't believe my ears. But there it was. And from that day onwards the indulgence of one cigarette was granted to Colonel Jimmy, but never to anyone else. Grandmother was really and truly allergic to tobacco smoke. It was no fad. After he had taken his leave, bells were rung, maids summoned, windows opened, curtains shaken, even fans were employed to get the horrid smell out of the room. It was grandmother's way of showing her gratitude.

To me Jimmy was, quite simply, my best friend. I could ask him things I would never have dreamed of asking father. It was Jimmy, not my parents, who guided me through the treacherous shoals of puberty and adolescence with a sanity and common sense for which I can never be too grateful. The idea of a friendship between a boy of ten and a man past sixty may seem ridiculous on the face of it, but there it was, solid as a rock and unshakable. He was quite undemanding. When I went to school he never expected me to write to him. Occasional postal orders would reach me, invariably towards the end of term when, as Jimmy well knew, pocket-money was at its lowest ebb, with a brief injunction not to make a beast of myself or bother him with letters and he had been round in 97. What did I think of that? But I always knew that when I went home Jimmy would listen to my problems, growl a word or two and, presto . . . the problems were problems no longer.

My last recollection of Jimmy was on an early September evening of 1914. He was sitting in his big armchair surrounded by his shining collection of trophies and looking rather frail. War had broken out, and by means of some contriving and string-pulling, I had become a trumpeter on the HQ staff of an artillery brigade. I was a very unofficial trumpeter, quite unable to blow a note, let alone a call, on any trumpet whatsoever. But that, as an infinitely greater than I used to remark, is another story. I was on embarkation leave before sailing for France.

'Tell you one thing, Donald,' rumbled Jimmy, 'You'll be scared when you come under fire. Bound to be, unless you've the hide of an alligator. But so'll everyone else. Don't forget that. Bein' afraid don't matter a damn so long's you don't show it. Fear's a bloody thing. Infectious. Never show it.'

At that time it just hadn't occurred to me that other people might be frightened in battle, and I was eaten up by the fear of being afraid. As always, Jimmy's pronouncement seemed to put things in their proper perspective, and when, a fortnight or so later, I first saw and heard German shells bursting around the battery, I remembered that being afraid, and I was, just didn't matter.

Jimmy died in 1916. By that time I had been commissioned to a new army brigade. We had a pretty gruelling time at Gallipoli. Dysentery and jaundice were worse enemies than the Turk ever was. We were brought up to strength in Egypt, rested in the desert east of the Canal and shipped over to France, where remounts were waiting for us, just in time for the Somme. The day mother's letter reached me, I had been detailed to go over to corps head-quarters and try to wring two new guns from the ordnance officer to replace a section of ours which were badly worn. Happily the ordnance officer turned out to be an old fishing acquaintance

– we had first met on the banks of the Awe – and that helped. Our business was most satisfactorily concluded, a rare happening in those days of shortages, and was followed by an invitation to lunch in the HQ mess. We discussed mutual friends in Argyll, but my thoughts were wandering. Over coffee my host said, 'For a young feller who's got all he asked for, you seem a bit down in the mouth. Anything wrong?'

I apologised and told him that an old friend in Oban had just died. A Colonel MacLeod, Jimmy MacLeod.

The corps commander, a distinguished Indian cavalry man, pricked up his ears. 'Did you say Jimmy MacLeod?'

'Yes, sir.'

'Wonder if he was the man I knew. Teetotaller who looked like a confirmed drunkard and rode like an archangel. Wonderful horseman. Never knew a better. More than that. When the turf over there wasn't just as clean as it ought to have been, MacLeod set an example to every rider in the country. He never rode a crooked race in his life.'

It was just the kind of epitaph that would have best pleased Colonel Jimmy.

# The First Salmon

SALMO SALAR is a noble fish. Even though he, or she, lacks the fighting fury of the sea trout. He, or – let's stick to the masculine gender – he is, in relation to his smaller cousin, regarded as a peer to a commoner, as a senator to a congressman. In Scotland, a salmon is quite simply a 'fish'.

'Did ye get a fish?' doesn't mean 'Did you get a trout?' Or a greyling or a sea trout or a cod or a mackerel. It means 'Did you catch a salmon?', just as, in Gaelic, *uisge* means water and *the* water is therefore whisky.

Three creatures cropped up more frequently in conversation round our dinner-table than upon it, and they seldom appeared physically, less often than twice a week during the appropriate seasons: the red deer, the salmon and the grouse. Grandfather, a really dedicated fisherman, the only one I ever knew who made his own greenheart rods, never cast a fly he hadn't tied himself. He might occasionally condescend to the use of a prawn, but spinning he despised. Worm he would allow when the water was right. But all in all he was a fly fisherman and equally deadly with dry and wet flies. Shooting he affected to despise.

Father, a first-rate performer with the shotgun and almost, if not quite, in the same class with a rifle, would pretend to look down upon all fishermen as a race overgiven to braggadocio and down-right lying.

The truth was that grandfather was a shocking bad shot and father never had the patience and cunning essential to the good fly fisherman.

So I both had my cake and ate it. No boy ever had better or more thorough tuition in both forms of sport.

It was strange to owe one's first fish to a Campbell, but that is how it came about. At a party of some sort, Mrs Campbell of Inverawe asked me, fifteen years old at the time, whether I had ever caught a salmon. I had not, in the sense she intended, but I had 'taken' a salmon in Lachie's company from strictly private and well-policed water, not hers.

'Then it's high time you did,' said kind Mrs Campbell, who owned some of the best pools on the Awe and promised to write about a day on her water in the approaching spring.

'Remember what I've taught you,' wrote grandfather in his tiny, rather Gothic, script, when advised of the coming event. 'Take the line back as high as you can and give it time to straighten out before you cast forward. And don't pay any attention to what your gillie tells you.' Which was all very well for grandfather, who only had to glance at a pool once to know instinctively where the fish would lie and how to approach them. And, at that time, he had not met Donald Struthers, the gillie who was appointed to look after me on the day. Donald belonged to a family which was not as surprising in the Highlands as it would be anywhere else. He was the youngest of three brothers. The eldest farmed, like his father before him, a small farm, not much more than a croft, near Dunstaffnage Castle. The second brother was a KCB, a high-ranking civil servant in the Department of Education, and Donald, the gillie, was the third. Sassenachs enjoying Mrs Campbell's hospitality would be dumbfounded to discover that the little leather-bound book Donald read, while they were munching their sandwiches at lunch-time, was a New Testament in Greek or, maybe, Book V of the 'Iliad'. Virgil and Horace he took in his stride, and for really light reading he preferred, of all things, 'Rasselas, Prince of Abyssinia', but only in one of his rare moods of frivolity. He once confided to me that the only Latin poet he might have made a fisher of was Horace, because he 'thought more like a chentleman than the others'.

Donald was a tall, thin man, clean shaven in a whiskery age, and melancholy. In fact, a scholar *manqué*. But he knew and loved his job. He was exquisitely courteous and beautifully mannered: both courtesy and manners were founded on the very proper conviction that he was the equal of any man breathing. They had nothing in common with the tip-hunting servility of indoor servants. He, for instance, could never have been guilty of what an Irish gillie once said to the Jam Sahib of Nawangar – 'Ranji' to every schoolboy who ever handled a cricket-bat. Ranji rented a beat on the Shannon one season. One day a fish took him greedily and tore away downstream, ripping the line off a screaming reel. The Irishman was fluent with advice: 'Take him easy now, your Highness, not too much of the butt now, let him have his head, your Highness, you have all the line you need. That's the way, your Highness, we'll have this one, it's well hooked he is.' The fish jumped. 'Drop the point, your Highness . . . drop the point!' Then the line slackened. The fish had gone. 'Ye black bastard, ye've lost him!'

We drove down in a dogcart to a bothy on the north bank and got ready to fish. Donald examined my tackle carefully; rod, reel, line, casts and flybook. (Grandfather had been at some pains, not to say expense, to make sure that my gear would pass muster.) He put the cast to soak in a puddle while he put up the rod, fixed the reel and threaded the line through the rings. Then he said very deliberately, 'You mustn't be expecting too much aal at once, Master Donald. It's too bright as yet and I'd sooner see the wind a bittie more to the south. But maybe after our lunch the weather will be changing.'

The Awe near Inverawe is a deep river, and in high water it can be dangerous. It is not wide, but the banks are rocky and in places precipitous. Wearing waders and brogues, hot, clumsy things to walk about in, one had to clamber and wade alternately to reach the various vantage points from which the pools could be properly fished. By lunch-time the day had provided some good casting practice, and I must have climbed what in the aggregate amounted to a small Alp, but no fish took the slightest interest in the 'Thunder and Lightning' presented for inspection.

Donald followed my erratic course at a higher level which enabled him to see down into the water and, perhaps, warn me of a rise. But nothing rose.

Backs to a warm granite rock, we lunched leisurelywise and looked up into a blue sky flecked by small cotton-woolly clouds drifting slowly overhead. To our left, Ben Cruachan rose majestically, dwarfing his vassal hills. Donald lit his pipe and, as the grey smoke curled up, he said, 'Maybe, if the fish are not rising, we could find a trout or two. I have some trout flies with me.'

It was his way of hinting that the day, as far as salmon were concerned, was a washout. But no . . . a thousand times no! On my first day's lawful salmon-fishing, salmon I would fish. Nothing less would do. We got up. Donald collected the wrappings and débris of the picnic meal, burned them behind a boulder, stamped out the fire and we went back to the river.

I had not then learned what incalculable creatures salmon are. The salmon flies of everyday use, the Jock Scott, Thunder and Lightning, Silver Doctor, to take three of the commonest (and the most successful), do not in the least resemble anything a fish is likely to see in the water. Yet they all kill fish. Some years later, fishing in Glen Etive with my host of a week-end, a strange thing happened. We started at the top of his water and fished down towards the loch, taking alternate pools as we went. Both of us were fairly experienced and successful fishermen. Neither of us got anything for our pains, not a rise. Having agreed to call it a day we walked back to the lodge. On the way we passed my host's daughter, a six-year-old, fishing away by herself. She was using a bamboo, seven or eight feet long, with a piece of string tied on firmly to the thinner end. Attached to the string were six inches of gut with a big hook baited with a piece of orange-peel. Just as we passed her there was a loud yell. Her bait had been taken by a fresh run grilse of four pounds weight. Among us we contrived to land it, but not until a spirited twenty minutes had elapsed and almost everyone including the angler, had fallen into the water, which was shallow.

When that kind of thing happens, one is more or less driven to the conclusion that sheer bloody-mindedness or plain bad temper, one or the other, impels the salmon to take a fly. If this theory is heretical, it is at least an empirical heresy.

As we went back to the water, Donald had another look at the weather and shook his head. We were near the western end of the Pass of Brander where, in the thirteenth century, a savage battle was fought between the Bruce and the MacDougalls. Here the MacDougalls of Dunollie won their most treasured heirloom, the Brooch of Lorne, wrenched from the plaid of Robert Bruce himself. It is a wild, narrow pass and the river runs fast and deep through the gorge, the brown water creaming round points of jagged rock which break the surface here and there.

We went to work in the same way as before, Donald some feet above me and behind, looking down into the water. Suddenly he gave a shout and came tumbling down the brae.

'Try you there again,' he said. 'Chust below the big rock. I could not be sure of it, but I think there was movement under the water.'

I cast again and dropped the fly in the same place as before. There was a boil in the water and a sharp tug at the line. There was no need to strike, the fish did it for me.

'Take in your line,' said Donald; 'quickly, now.'

The fish headed towards us, thought better of it, turned back, and the fight was on.

Anglers should give thanks nightly for the fact that salmon do not know their own strength. If they did, they would never be taken by rod and line. I was reasonably strong for my age, the rod was a fifteen-foot split cane from Hardy of Alnwick, a powerful thing, most beautifully balanced; yet at first I had the sensation of being caught by something far more powerful than I was. Then he dived and sulked at the bottom of the pool for a few minutes.

'Keep the strain on him,' said Donald. 'Chust keep the strain and by and by we will see what he will be after.'

So far, neither of us had seen our enemy. Then, suddenly, the strain was gone, the line went slack and my heart leapt into my mouth. The fish jumped clear out of the water.

'Lower your point!' shouted the gillie.

For a split second the great fish hung in the air, then fell back into the water with a crash and a splash of spray. Next second the rod was nearly torn out of my hands. He was still hooked.

'By God,' said Donald, who never took his Maker's name in vain, or not in my hearing, 'By God, that iss a fish you have there!'

One account of playing a fish is, I know only too well, very much like another, although no two salmon behave alike. Luck held, the line held, but soon my arms were aching and I had no reason to believe that the salmon had begun to tire.

'Look you, Master Donald,' said the gillie; 'this iss a fish we must not loose, maybe you will never see his like in aal your days.' He spoke prophetically although he knew it not. 'If you become too tired I will take the rod from you if you wish, but I am thinking you would prefer to bring the fish to bank by your-self. Don't be giving him too much of the butt, now. Chust a steady strain, and rest yourself when you can.'

That salmon fought like a demon. He tried quick, short rushes, he skulked at the bottom of the pool, he nearly as possible broke me on a rock. It took all my strength and Donald's know-how to stop him getting out of the pool into a shallow, stony run which linked it with the pool below. Twice again he jumped, and each time looked bigger, and fresher, than before.

Forty-five minutes, they felt like as many hours, passed before Donald's strategy began to take effect, and, for the first time in that afternoon, I began to feel that I and not the fish was in control. Twice I brought him in to the bank, but not close enough for Donald's gaff. But the third time the gaff flashed, quick and sure. Two minutes after that he was dangling on Donald's pocket-scales, all thirty-five and a half pounds of him, a great cock fish, fresh from the sea with the sea lice still on him. Thirty-five and a half pounds. Mere numerals do not do justice to such a fish. For fifty years since that day, from time to time, in various waters, I have tried to catch his like, but never came within twenty pounds of him. I never shall. Even now, as those words go down, it is with the private hope that the gods will see them and some day, out of sheer perversity, prove them wrong.

Mother, who knew the form, had packed a silver flask filled with whisky in my fishing-bag.

'Not for you, of course, but in case you have to give the gillie a dram.' Out it came, I pulled the cup off the bottom of the flask, filled it, and handed it to Donald with some very, very inadequate words of thanks. Before tasting it, he looked at me and said slowly, 'I am thinking, Master Donald, that you would be the better of a drop yourself. It iss rather young you are for the whisky, but . . . see here.'

He produced one of those collapsible metal cups from his pocket, opened it out, half filled it from the flask and we toasted each other, my first silver fish and my first golden dram in one and the same magical moment. Donald smiled, wiped his mouth with the back of his hand and said, 'I will not be telling anyone.'

Long afterwards he told me that I was looking so white and exhausted – 'the freckles standing out on your face like beech leaves on snow' – that he wouldn't have been surprised if he had to carry me as well as the fish all the way to Inverawe House.

We reached the 'big hoose' as dusk was falling and the maids were lighting the lamps in the hall. One of them went to tell Mrs Campbell that we were back. Meanwhile Donald laid the salmon on a marble-topped hall table that had carried many hundreds of fish before that day, but seldom a bigger.

People seemed to pour out of the drawing-room; there were feminine cries of admiration, masculine growls of envy; the fish was weighed again, measured, and entered in the book.

Then there was tea in the dining-room specially for me. The others had had theirs. A no-nonsense, Argyllshire kind of tea with soda scones, potato scones, piping hot and swimming in fresh, melted butter, with oatcakes and heather honey, home-made jam, rich fruit cake, shortbread and admiration, something I never seemed to taste at home. It was Heaven, it was triumph. It was almost celebrity. (That came later when the 'Oban Times' reported my fish and the 'Field' reprinted it when I had gone back to school. The housemaster found the account there, cut it out and pinned the cutting on the board, so everybody knew about it.)

Then Mrs Campbell said it would be a shame to cut up such a salmon before father and mother had seen it, so she had given orders for it to be sewn into a bass and put in the back of the dogcart, and if I liked, I could have a cast made by Mr Bisshop the Oban taxidermist. Anyhow, it was to be all mine to do what I liked with.

I began to think differently about Campbells from that day onward.

One of the men of the party said it was a pity that such a fish couldn't be celebrated in a dram, what did Mrs Campbell think? Mrs Campbell promptly thought that my father and mother wouldn't approve at all, and just at that moment Donald came into the hall to say that the fish and my gear had been packed and that Major had been harnessed. He heard Mrs Campbell and gave me a great, slow wink from his long, solemn face and I nearly giggled out loud.

Happiness is a relative condition, but I don't think I was ever happier in my whole life than during the drive back from Inverawe to Oban. It was a soft, spring night, warm and moonlit. Old Major, the elder of our two carriage horses, the other was called Minor, trotted along at a good clip, the prospects of his own warm stable ahead and the bran mash, with a bottle of Guinness in it, which always followed any night work. The carriage-lamps flickered, lighting drystone dykes and hedges rather than the road.

And the euphoria was not over. There would be more to come. The pleasure of wiring grandfather and waiting for his answer; mother's delight; Mrs O'Callaghan's rhapsodies and father's quiet approval. Oh, life was very, very good!

# The First King

NOBODY ever explained to me just how it came about. It could have been grandfather, who was a friend of Sir Charles Cust who . . . but it might be wiser to start from the beginning.

Most small boys are natural braggarts. In the locker-room at school this kind of thing was common conversational coin:

A: 'My pater's just bought a new pair of chestnuts for the carriage.'

B: 'How many horses have you got?'

A: 'Four. Why?'

B: 'We have seven, not counting my pony.'

C: 'Bet my Uncle William has more than both of you put together. He hunts.'

A: and B. 'Nobody asked you about your smelly old Uncle William, so shut up.'

C: 'Won't shut up. He has. I'll bet you.'

A: 'Bet what?'

C: 'Stick of chocolate.'

And so forth and so forth. All I could brag about in such exchanges (we only kept Major, Minor, and my pony Morag) was father's shooting. It was perfectly true that, on the occasions I had been allowed to go out with him, I had never known him to miss a shot at feather or fur. I had not then seen him shoot at driven birds from a butt or stand. But it was obvious, to me at least, that if he brought down everything he fired at, he must be the best shot in Argyllshire. But why stop there? The best in the Highlands, the best in Scotland, the best in Britain, the best in the world. It was simple as that.

# The First King

There was among us one rather sophisticated bratling whose father reared pheasants on his broad and rich acres in the Border country and dukes came cheerfully to shoot them. The bratling's photograph once appeared in the 'Tatler' between his father and the then Duke of Roxburghe, both bristling with guns. On the strength of this, the Ram, a nickname derived from his initials, became an authority. Once he took me aside.

'I say, Dumps.' (My horrible nickname.)

'Yes?'

'I wouldn't say things like that about your pater.'

'Things like what?'

'That he's the best shot in the world. Because he isn't.'

'How do you know?'

'I asked my pater last holidays. He'd never even heard of your pater and he knows absolutely everybody. He says that Lord de Grey and the Prince of Wales are the best shots in the country, and he's shot with both of them.'

'Bet he hasn't shot with everybody. Bet he hasn't shot in the Highlands. My pater never misses anything. Nobody can shoot better than that.'

This logic, backed by personal and passionate conviction, carried the day.

'Well . . . I don't know for certain,' he wavered. 'But . . . oh, come on, let's bowl at a stump.' And we did that.

I became very, very curious about the experts he named, and wanted more than anything on earth to see them in action. But I continued to brag till almost every boy in the school believed me. Such is the reward of repetition. New boys were told:

'That's Dumps. But don't you call him that. Warts don't use nicknames in their first term. He'll clout you if you do. His pater's the best shot in the country.'

Other persons, better able to judge and less partisan, came to know about father. Invitations to shoot came from places far beyond the borders of Argyll. King Edward died and the Prince of Wales became King George V. His bearded profile supplanted that of his father on our coins and stamps (but looked in a different direction), and now I wanted to see the King shoot. I told everybody.

Each year we spent the latter part of August and the beginning of September with grandfather in the Parsonage at Fasque in Kincardineshire. Sometimes mother was with me, sometimes father, but seldom both at the same time. The visiting season was on and we kept the Oban house open, if only for grandmother's sake, all the year round.

The Parsonage was a square, comfortable old house built of granite with no architectural pretensions whatsoever. The front door was flanked by two windows and surmounted by three more. It faced south, and on the west side lay a big garden, my Aunt Lucy's especial charge. In front were two long, narrow lawns divided by a carriage drive, and the whole was enclosed by copper-beech hedges. A huge copper beech overshadowed the east gable, and, on the other lawn, directly opposite, there was a fine weeping willow-tree.

Grandfather's study overlooked the garden and he had a wooden outside staircase built up the side of the house to his window. It was not a fire-escape so much as a bishop-escape. When unwelcome visitors called, grandfather could conceal himself behind the sweet-peas in less time than it takes to put this on paper.

Beyond and about the garden lay the wide, timbered park of Fasque, Sir John Gladstone's house, and close by was an artificial lake well stocked with brown and rainbow trout. Grandfather, who had been at Eton with Sir John, had the freedom of park and lake alike. He had his own key to the boat-house and kept a rod there permanently. Grandfather could be in a boat on the lake, rod in hand and absorbed in the business of fishing within twenty minutes of the first ring at the door-bell.

But grandfather deserves some explanation. I hope this may be worthy of him. In build and general appearance he was not unlike King Edward VII. Perhaps he wore his beard rather more closely clipped. His eyes were bluer and less protrusive and he weighed three stones less than the King. How he came to take Holy Orders, I do not know. It was not, at any rate, from any financial compulsion. I don't suppose he ever wore a ready-made garment in his life. His clothes came from Savile Row, his boots from Lobb and his wine from Justerini & Brooks. He never paid less than three figures for a horse. He was no dedicated priest and he certainly was no preacher. He used, just as they came, some thirty sermons which he had adapted from volumes published by eighteenth-century divines, and read one each Sunday to his long-suffering congregation. His system was to 'cut the theology, keep the commonsense and use language understood of the people'.

I think his feeling towards the hierarchy of the Church approximated to that experienced by an intelligent, amateur subaltern to a stuffy professional colonel. But, if he dispensed smallish beer from the pulpit to his parishioners, he looked after their material needs and their general welfare with unceasing watchfulness. His purse was always open to the needy, his larder and cellar to the hungry, if they were not bishops. (Who ever heard of a hungry bishop?) He never tried to understand the Scot, he accepted him and made the best of him. To me, grandfather was Sir Oracle.

Every Friday the maids put together a queer contraption in his study. There were four walls of a waterproof material surrounding a chair beneath which some kind of heating apparatus was placed. It raised steam. There was a hole in the lid of this box for grandfather's head, and when the lid was shut, there he sat, growing pinker and pinker as the steam grew hotter and hotter, and looking like some conjuring trick from a Maskelyne and Devant show at the Egyptian Hall. He liked me to come and listen to him talk during this weekly boiling. He was a classical scholar of considerable attainments, and really more at home with Terence or Plautus than the good bishops whose sermons he pirated. His study was lined with books all the way round, and I was made free of them, with the exception of one small bookcase which he kept locked. It was not for many years, not, in fact, till after his death that we discovered it to contain Ruff's 'Guide to the Turf' and all that was most recent and reliable on the breeding, running and training of blood-stock.

Grandfather was an excellent corrective. He made me read, and appreciate, Sir Walter Scott, but when he found that Sir Walter, to say nothing of Sir Arthur Conan Doyle, had filled my noddle with exaggerated ideas about chivalry, he corrected that with a copy of 'Don Quixote'. He compelled me to criticise. It was never enough to say that one liked or disliked a book, one had to say why, which led to clear thinking. You never dared to be slipshod with grandfather. One summer, when I was only eleven, he read Gibbon with me. Next term at school, the head-master was stunned and amazed by my erudition.

He was as fastidious about food and wine as he was about his linen and fishing-tackle. Dinner at the Parsonage was a ceremony conducted by two tablemaids with seemly ritual and excellent cooking. He too had an Irish cook, but she was no Mrs O'Callaghan, as grandfather was ready to admit. She was a dry, shrivelled little creature who referred to grandfather as 'his Holy Riverence'. To grandfather, when the soufflé was all it should have been, she was 'that excellent Mrs Kelly', or 'the Popish poisoner' when things went wrong.

Mother, his eldest daughter and heiress, in the genealogical sense, inherited her pride of family from grandfather. His was a peripatetic family, inclining to become admirals, colonial governors and judges, and even polar explorers, since the time of Charles II. One of them left his books to the infant Princeton University to form the nucleus of a library, and modern Princeton commemorates the gift by a carving of our arms over the present library door. Grandfather's only son Charles was a midshipman in the Royal Navy when he was killed in the Boxer Rising, but not before he contrived to send home some Eastern souvenirs. In the drawing-room there was a good red-and-gold lacquer cabinet, some Chinese paintings on silk, and what Lord Tennyson, rather elaborately, called 'laborious orient ivory sphere in sphere' inside a glass dome on the mantelpiece. That I was never allowed to touch, and so never discovered just how many spheres within spheres there really were.

One day at breakfast grandfather looked at me over his 'Times'. Typically, he preferred to read 'The Times' newspaper a day late, rather than the 'Glasgow Herald' or 'Scotsman' of the day. Twenty-four hours one way or another made little difference to the ordered leisure of his course.

'Your father's coming this afternoon. He's going to murder small birds at Glendye. Like to go with him?'

The question was perfectly redundant and we both knew it. I nodded.

'Grandfather?'

'Yes, boy.'

'Will it be a drive?'

'Good gracious, boy; of course it will. You'll see some really good shooting for a change.'

'None of them will be better than father.'

'You will see for yourself.'

He winked at mother who asked, would-be-casualwise:

'Will he be there?'

Grandfather nodded and plunged again into the columns of 'The Times'. Obviously something was up, but I was too well trained to ask questions.

The weather, that autumn, was halcyon. In the afternoon we had tea out of doors under the weeping willow, which afforded a green shade without cutting off the little breeze there was.

'Donald,' said grandfather, 'you mustn't harp. It becomes boring. By now we all know that you want to see the King shoot. But why should you? The King doesn't want to see you. He probably doesn't know that you exist.' I thought about that and it did seem barely possible. 'Moreover,' grandfather continued, 'you wouldn't know what to do if you did meet him.'

'Is it different from meeting . . . Lord Strathcona?'

'Quite different,' said grandfather. 'To begin with, you don't speak to the King unless he speaks to you first, or asks you a question. What would you call the King if you did happen to meet him?'

'Sire?' I had been reading Dumas.

'No. Wrong again. The first time he speaks to you, you call him "your Majesty". After that, you call him "sir" until he dismisses you. Then, when you bow, you say "your Majesty" again. Have you got that in your head?'

'I think so.'

'Do you know how to make a bow?'

'Like this?'

I jumped up, bun in hand, jack-knifed from the waist down and shot up again. Grandfather was horrified.

'No, no, no! That's entirely wrong. Now watch me.'

Grandfather got up from his wicker chair and stood straight. Then he bowed his head and shoulders very slightly and straightened up.

'There,' he said. 'Like that. You want to show respect, not agility. Now do you know what to do?'

'Yes, Grandfather. Thank you. Oh . . .'

'What is it?'

'Why did you show me all this today?'

'Because it is something you ought to know and because it is something you will not learn at school. Every gentleman should learn the respect due to his King and the form it should take.'

Then the carriage, with father inside, turned into the drive and we all got up from the tea-table and went to meet him.

Next morning father and I started off in the Parsonage trap at the crack of dawn. The comparative slowness of transport in those days often allowed one to see that forgotten and practically obsolete phenomenon, the sunrise. There were three of us in the trap, father, Custice, one of the Fasque grooms and my first Cockney, who was on loan to father as a loader, and I. Custice drove. Father would never, if he could avoid it, drive either horses or a motor-car before shooting. His theory was that the strain on the wrists affected his co-ordination. Years after, when playing tournament golf, I found that it was worth two or three putts in a day's play *not* to drive oneself to the course.

By half-past nine we were pulling up a steep hill with acres and acres of brownish-purple heather on either hand rolling away as far as one could see. We went up the Cairn-o'-Mount road past Spitalburn, crossed the Water o' Dye at the brig, and pulled into the side of the road at a high point beyond the Glendye Lodge where several other people and their transport were already assembled.

Mother had been rather tiresome about my clothes the night before. She insisted on the 'good' kilt, which came between my everyday kilt and the Sunday-best horror, and the 'good' kilt jacket with a tie and tackety shoes. By now it was almost ten o'clock, growing hot too, but all my attempts to shed the tie were sternly frustrated.

From where we stood, one could look back along the road we had travelled, or northwards where one could see its ribbon unroll across heathery shoulders in the direction of Kincardine O'Neil. Father was greeted by our host and carried off to meet those among the guns he did not already know, while I sat on a stone dyke and remembered that small boys should be seen but not heard. There was lots going on. There were the underkeepers with the dogs, there were loaders assembling their masters' guns, filling cartridge-bags from magazines. Four horses had been unharnessed from two shooting-brakes and blanketed while enjoying their nosebags. A boy not much older than me was walking a saddled garron up and down, and the head-keeper, with rolled red and green flags under his tweedy arm, conferred with Sir John.

A tall, soldierly kind of man, with a clipped moustache and leather patches on the shoulders of his jacket, came and talked to me, but I was too excited inside for conversation. This was my first sight of a grouse-drive. Another man came to join him.

'Think he's goin' to be late?' asked the second.

The first man laughed. 'You know as well as I do that he's never late. There you are! I won't say "talk of the Devil", that would hardly be respectful, but there he is.' The first man pointed towards Greendams, where a moving black speck, trailing a cloud of dust, showed on the white road.

Close on the stroke of ten, a big limousine drew up almost opposite where I was sitting. Now motor-cars were objects of enormous interest to me. Till then I had only seen four, and travelled three ecstatic miles in one before it broke down. I slipped off the wall to go and examine this one, which was the biggest I had seen. But suddenly the car was surrounded by people and all of them were carrying their hats in their hands. A footman opened the door and a short, bearded man in shooting-clothes got out and was met by our host. Then, as I saw him properly for the first time, my eyes nearly popped out of my head, and I had a quick look at my luck-piece, a Coronation five-shilling bit, which lived in my sporran. But before there was time for comparisons, father was beside me; father was bowing and shaking hands.

'Is this your boy?'

'Yes, your Majesty.'

The King smiled down at me and held out his hand. I took it, bowing in the manner laid down so carefully by grandfather.

'You're the boy who wants to see me shoot?'

I gulped, swallowed and nodded. 'Yes, your Majesty.'

'Well, that can be arranged. When we move off to the butts, you'd better follow my pony.'

'Yes, sir.' And he passed on to speak with others. Grandfather was wrong. The King had heard about me! But there was still a tinge of disappointment in my surprise. Not even I expected the King to shoot grouse in robes and a crown. But a tweed suit like anyone else? That didn't seem quite right. A field-marshal's uniform perhaps? 'Bobs', Lord Roberts of Kandahar, was one of my heroes and a picture of him stood on my dressing-table at home. Hastily visualising it, it became immediately obvious that nobody could shoot grouse in a field-marshal's long, patent-leather boots which reached above the knee.

Suddenly all the seemingly aimless activity all round became purposeful. The guns were allotted their butts. The dogs were leashed. The King mounted his pony and, with an under-keeper leading the way, the party moved off.

'Go ahead,' said father. 'You heard what the King told you.'

I trotted off and fell in beside the King's loader, who was carrying his guns and cartridge-bags. Sir John walked by the pony's head. We turned off the road and down a cart-track in the heather for about a mile before reaching the first line of butts.

For the first drive the King occupied the last butt on the extreme right flank of the line. Whether he drew for it as the other guns did, or whether it was allotted to him as the best position, I don't know. Anyhow, as the coveys came over, they tended to swing left-winged, down the slope where the King was waiting for them. The little wind there was and the lie of the land both combined to favour him. One by one the other guns occupied their own butts. Father was in six, the King in eight. When, at last, he dismounted, he went into the butt with his loader and had a look round. Just a little below and behind him were three big boulders. He signed to me.

'There,' he said; 'you'll be quite safe behind those stones. Do you fidget? I suppose you do. All boys fidget. But you mustn't. You must keep still. Understand?'

'Yes, sir.'

'If you move about, you'll catch my eye and put me off. Don't forget. No fidgeting. If you do, I'll – I'll have your head chopped off.'

We had been reading Tudor history in my last term at prep school, a period in which monarchs were always sending people to have their heads chopped off, and for one moment I . . . then I saw the King's smile. If he hadn't been the King, you might have called it a grin, and, anyhow, came the comforting reflection, father would never allow anyone to chop off my head. So I grinned back, went where I was bidden . . . and froze there. The King was smoking a Turkish cigarette and the aromatic smoke drifted past as he and his loader made their final preparations.

There is something about absolute mastery in any sport or game or art which is quite unmistakable when seen. 'Sovereign sway and masterdom', as Shakespeare called it, speaks for itself. The onlooker needs no knowledge of the game, art or sport to recognise it. I once took a French boy, who had never seen a cricket match, to Lord's. Two Gloucestershire wickets fell while I tried to explain the laws of cricket, and my guest was bored although he did his best to simulate interest. Then Walter Hammond came out of the pavilion and took guard. He played three balls carefully and easily, then drove the fourth like a red streak through the covers to the boundary. The French lad sat up.

'Now this one . . . he excels, does he not?'

'He's the best batsman in England.'

'*Cela se voit.*'

You don't need to be musical to recognise a master pianist when you hear one. The authority of absolutism comes through. It was enough to see Walter Hagen swing a club, and he was no stylist, to know you were in the presence of greatness. So it was with King George. Till that morning I had only seen good shots shooting well. But he was something very different. His judgment of speed and distance was flawless. He never had to take a chance. He was so fast that the long shot at the bird which may be just out of range never happened. There was no 'tailoring' and there were no wounded birds. Every bird he hit was stone dead before it hit the heather. Where most guns would be happy to pull off two rights and lefts, one in front of the butt and one behind, the King took five birds and made it look easy. A single shot at long range, change guns, take a right and left; then, with the first gun reloaded, another right and left behind. As for the clean miss, something that happens to the best of shots from time to time, well, he did not miss. I suppose that even he must have had an off day now and again, but it would be hard to imagine it.

Then it was all over. There was shouting in the distance, flags were waved, beaters hove in sight and the dogs went out to do their part. I unfroze. It had been a good beat and birds were plentiful. The head-keeper was happy, Sir John was happy, the King *was* a better shot than my father and I would have to admit it.

The King's pony was led up while the game was being collected and the guns prepared to move on to the next beat. He mounted and signalled to father, who came across to speak with him. Father looked happy too.

'Now, then,' said the King, 'I hope you weren't disappointed with me. Now, tell us. Which of us is the better shot?'

'You, sir.' It was dragged out of me.

Then he was merciful. 'Don't forget, shooting is a matter of practice. And I get much more practice than your father does.'

A great white light dawned upon me. Of course that was the explanation. Why hadn't I thought about it sooner?

The rest of the day was much like the beginning. There was a wonderful lunch: zinc-lined baskets of steaming, delicious Irish stew; cold grouse and salmon; trifles and jellies. Ladies in long tweed skirts with blackcock feathers in their hats drove out to join us, and they were just the same as other ladies and made silly remarks about my hair and growth and character, though they must have been much more fashionable than the ladies who made the same remarks in Oban. And the sun blazed and the clegs and horseflies came out and the ladies went in and we got back to the business in hand. During the last drive I was allowed to load for father because Curtice had to go back and harness the horse before we could go home.

Then there were good-byes and thanks and tips for the head-keeper and the loaders, and everyone was given a brace or two with Sir John's compliments. The King got into his Daimler and was driven back to Balmoral, and we trotted off in the opposite direction towards the Parsonage, and the moon was rising when we reached home.

Many years later, when I walked bareheaded through Westminster Hall, where the King lay in state beneath a purple pall, with the Crown, glittering with gems in the candlelight, on his coffin, watched by scarlet-and-gold officers from the Brigade of Guards, I thought less of the resounding titles, less of all that muted splendour, than of the kindly gentleman in tweeds who took care to save a schoolboy's 'face' on the moors of Glendye.

# The First Gun

TODAY, when walking down to the village, I am, as often as not, held up at the points of twin six-shooters, and very realistic guns they are, in the hands of a six-year-old.

He also carries a Robin Hood bow and a quiverful of arrows, thus making the best of two worlds; and, moreover, he possesses a passably noisy tommy-gun; that is when he hasn't run out of percussion caps. If one envies the quality of his toys – we had no such realism in our time – a certain misgiving creeps in anent the wisdom of allowing youngsters to 'shoot down' all and sundry even in play. Maybe it's just blimpishness on my part.

Human life has lost its high value after two holocausts in a quarter of a century, but it is unwise to generalise, and my misgivings are rooted in my upbringing.

Every countrybred boy longs for a gun of his own (generalisation again!), and I, most certainly, was no exception. Father's guns, a pair of hammerless ejectors by Purdey, built to measure and as exquisitely made as any chronometer, were sacrosanct. He never allowed anyone other than himself to clean or handle them.

No matter how late he got home after a day on the moor and a long drive back, the first thing he asked for was a kettle of boiling water. The barrels were washed out with the water, then cleaned with dry tow on the end of a ramrod which was renewed thrice, or as many times more as happened to be necessary, till the tow came out as clean as it went in. Then, lastly, a run-through with a drop of Rangoon oil on the tow. The stocks, trigger-guards, and any exposed metal were carefully cleaned and given a touch of oil on a dry rag, then the guns were cased and locked and put away. The routine never altered, even when he was staying in other houses where the custom was for keepers or loaders to take care of the guns. Even at Balmoral he insisted on cleaning his own, and the practice won King George's approval.

They were valuable guns; in those days you could pay about a hundred and eighty guineas for a pair of Purdeys, perhaps more if you wanted gold damascene work or inlaid crests or monograms on the walnut stocks. Three things, father said, should never be loaned to anybody in any circumstances whatsoever: a gun, a rifle and a toothbrush. Later on I added a pet trout-rod to that list, but father was not really interested in fishing and lent his rods to anyone who asked for them.

The first weapon to come my way which could possibly be described as lethal was the Gem air-gun so promptly confiscated after the shooting of John MacKechnie. It was a year before I got it back and by then it didn't matter much, because by dint of practice I had become fairly useful with a catapult, and both Lachie and I had killed (roosting) pheasants (and not my father's), by moonlight, with that weapon. A drain-pipe ran down past the bedroom window and it was easy to get out after the household had gone to bed. At first it was difficult to swarm up it again, but two midshipmen of the Royal Navy taught me how to do that in the right way.

One Christmas holiday father hired a twenty-bore for me from a local ironmonger, bought a box of fifty cartridges and took me for a prowl round our woods. Wisely, the dogs were left in the kennels. But for long before that, the laws of the Medes and the Persians were dinned into my thick head.

They were:

NEVER point a gun at anyone, even if you know it to be unloaded.

NEVER carry a gun in such a manner that it may possibly point at anyone.

Never carry a loaded gun at any time or in any place where you are not actually expecting to use it.

Never cross a dyke, ditch, fence, stile or hedge without first breaking your gun and taking out the cartridges.

Never fire at anything you cannot see clearly. Something brown moving in the bracken may be a hare or a rabbit, but it may be someone else's dog.

Never leave a gun loaded while you are lunching, or during any other break in the day's sport.

Never pull the trigger if you have any shadow of doubt in your mind that what you are firing at may be out of range. You want to be sure of killing. A gun who wounds birds or beasts is a bad gun.

Never, if you are shooting in company, forget the position of the guns on either side of you, and Never fire at their birds.

These laws were drilled into me till I hated the sound of them; I was cross-examined in them again and again and again. It was made crystal clear to me that a gun who was thought of as a bad risk to other guns simply wasn't asked to shoot. The result was that by degrees one observed the rules automatically and without having to think about them at all.

However strictly you yourself may have been brought up in this direction, it is never wise to assume that others have had a like education. That lesson was learned fairly early in my own experience and in a curious way. A friend from Perthshire was staying with us. It was a hard winter, and John MacKechnie the gardener reported that woodcock had been seen at no great distance from the house in a little hollow where there was a small natural spring which seldom froze up completely. My father suggested to our friend that they should look round and see what was doing. They came back with two and a half brace.

Returning home from a week-end at Benderloch, I went in by the back yard, having visited the stables. Father's study had a door which opened onto the yard, and by the door, leaning up against the wall, was a double-barrelled shotgun. Guns of any kind will draw any countrybred boy at any time, so I picked it up and put it to my shoulder, aiming at an imaginary high pheasant. I then put both fingers on the triggers and did it again. Both barrels immediately went off . . . *bang-bang* . . . almost simultaneously. Luckily no damage was done. Except to me. It was the one and only occasion when I questioned the justice of punishment. It would never have so much as occurred to me that anyone could in any circumstances leave a loaded gun propped up against a wall, let alone with the safety-catch off. That our friend used a very light pull was just more bad luck. He was no longer a friend of mine. Those who broke the rules seemed major criminals to me. For broken they certainly were. It is extraordinary how careless quite experienced guns can be.

That twenty-bore was a horrible gun; a cheap, mass-produced thing from a Belgian factory. It was badly balanced, too short in the stock and it didn't even throw straight. But it was quite undeniably a gun, and the first time I put it under my arm and went out with half a dozen cartridges in my pocket, I wouldn't have changed places with the King of England. I fired five shots that afternoon, four at rabbits and one at a woodcock and hit nothing at all. Nothing. And one of those rabbits would have been a dead snip with a catapult. Coming home with my tail between my legs was humiliating.

But next day a queer-looking mechanism was delivered at the house, together with a barrel. The barrel was full of black saucers packed in straw. It was a trap and some clay pigeons. It didn't take father half a dozen shots to find out what was the matter with the gun. It went back to the ironmonger. In its place came a single-barrelled 16-bore with a hammer, from a decent gunmaker. If held straight it was an effective, hard-hitting weapon. There is something to be said for training a youngster with a single barrel. If he knows he must hit with the first shot and has no second barrel to fall back upon, it will better his shooting. I liked that gun and didn't often miss with it. I even begged father to buy it for me, but he shook his head. That was hard to understand, because he always believed that a good workman deserved good tools. At the time when Lord Roberts was running a single-handed campaign to shatter the country's complacency *vis-à-vis* Germany, he demanded that every boy should learn how to handle a rifle. The schools took him at his word and instituted shooting competitions. The smaller boys used the powerful and accurate BSA air-rifle which was remarkably good at short ranges. We fired at twenty-five yards at targets with bulls supposed to approximate to the normal bull at 200, 500 and 600 yards respectively. Shooting for the Eight in a competition against fifty other preparatory schools, I had a good day and turned in three targets, each a possible. Twenty-one bulls in twenty-one shots. This feat was rewarded by a treasured letter from the Field-Marshal himself and a silver cup for the school. Father instantly scrapped the Gem, gave me a BSA of my own and, next year, a .22 long Greener target-rifle. He never believed that 'anything is good enough for a child'. He never grudged new golf-clubs, cricket-bats or tennis-rackets, as long as they were the best to be had, and he himself never used anything but the best available. I have never had any doubt that a boy with a good new bat will face the bowling with far more confidence than one who has to use last year's cracked, bound and chipped old warrior.

But in this instance it was 'No', and one didn't argue or whine about father's decisions, one accepted them, and continued to use the hireling *qua* hireling.

Before going back to school that autumn, we had a competition. Each of us started with twenty-five cartridges and as many clay pigeons. John set and sprung the trap for us. Father was not allowed to use more than one barrel. Mother refereed. At the final reckoning, father, of course, had broken all twenty-five of his 'birds' and there were twenty-three to my credit. That was considered good enough for one of tender years, and thereafter I was formally licensed to go out by myself, unsupervised, or with a dog, when game was wanted for the pot. Within our own policies shooting for shooting's sake was not encouraged, but what with gun-dogs, the West Highland terriers Shunach and Nollaig, the cats, and some dozen human beings to feed, there was always a use for rabbits and the odd pheasant, duck or woodcock. There was plenty of practice. And that particular brand of rough shooting is the best training a youngster can have. He must be on his toes all the time and take his chances within a split second or come back empty handed.

In that year school broke up two days before Christmas Eve. The house had been decorated with holly and evergreens and there were six inches of snow on the ground. The bay and the Sound of Mull were leaden grey and the white blanketing made the hills look even higher than usual. In fact, it was Ye Olde Worlde Yuletide, a thing which doesn't seem to happen any more in these British Isles. One knows that Henry VIII could and did travel from York House, now Whitehall, to his palace at Greenwich by sleigh, horse-drawn over a solid Thames. Charles II and James his brother presided over the roasting of an ox, whole, on the ice before Whitehall one New Year, but these picturesque things don't happen any more. We seldom have frost enough to freeze the village duckpond. But that year it was a white Christmas, despite the Gulf Stream which washed our Western Islands and warmed our sea lochs.

We had a family Christmas code. One was never supposed to display any curiosity about one's Christmas presents or so much as mention them. In theory, some last-minute delinquency could cancel them altogether. In practice, one could usually wring some secret information from Mrs O'Callaghan or Maggie. But that year security was unusually effective. The best to be got from them was that there was 'something in a box, a long flat boxie' for me. There was always a sharp distinction drawn between 'hard' presents and 'soft' presents. 'Soft' presents implied socks, mufflers, knitted pullovers and disappointingly utilitarian things of that nature. 'Hard' presents were twice as interesting. At least the 'boxie' was hard.

There was a devilish practice at my school which made it obligatory for each boy to take home his end-of-term report personally and hand it to his parent or guardian. At home this ceremony took place after dinner on the first night of the holidays and was got over as quickly as possible. It was apt to be embarrassing to all parties concerned. Not that my reports were so bad; all in all, they were pretty good, and I had taken a fair share of school prizes. But there was the insuperable fact that mathematics were beyond my scope. Father and mother, as in duty bound, would pounce upon this weakness and read me a lecture about want of trying hard, assuring me that maths were not intrinsically difficult and that anyone who really worked hard at them could master the subject. Knowing very well that mother could never make the household accounts balance properly and that father had the strongest possible aversion to any kind of calculation or adding up of figures, this jawbation was accepted ritually in the spirit which inspired it and immediately forgotten.

While it was in progress before the smoking-room fire, my attention strayed to the glass-fronted cupboard which contained odd weapons, mostly mine. Air-guns, air-rifles, target-rifles, air-pistols and a collector's gun for shooting small birds with dust-shot. It was never used, there was no ammunition for it and nobody knew how it had got there (although I had to keep it clean). Then I suddenly realised that the hireling wasn't there.

'Pay attention, Donald,' said mother, 'your father's talking to you!'

'Yes, mother . . . sorry!'

What father was saying I never really took in, because my mind was filled with the horrible thought that the Christmas holidays were here and that there would be invitations to shoot with Colonel MacDougall of MacDougall at Dunollie, and there would be woodcock as well as pheasants in the Dunollie woods, with Harry MacDonald of Dunach, and that there would probably be days at home, at Soroba, at Letterwalton, even at Achnacone . . . and there was no gun for me. NO GUN.

But it didn't seem the right moment to bring up the matter.

Christmas Eve meant that the whole household would be hard at work all day and that we would go to a Christmas Carol Service in St John's Church in the evening. Oban took very varying views of Christmas in those days. For us Episcopalians and for adherents of the old religion, Christmas was a major festival. The Presbyterians also looked upon it as a religious feast but on a different scale. In their view candles, trees and decorations wore a suspect popish aura and there was overmuch pandering to the gratification of the flesh. But even the very narrowest Wee Free was also apt to be a husband and a father, and his principles were seldom strong enough to deny his ain bairns the shortbread, black bun, ginger wine, conversation lozenges, crackers, presents and other good things enjoyed by the followers of the Scarlet Woman who lived next door. So the half of us kept our Christmas wholeheartedly and the others kept it surreptitiously behind drawn curtains, making their children the excuse for all the extras that found their way into house and cottage at that time of year. And if their attitude did, to some small extent, impair the general atmosphere of goodwill, all differences would soon be washed away in the flood of good whisky poured out for Hogmanay—a festival far, far older than the Christian Churches and somewhat frowned upon by all of them.

All that is now very much a thing of the past. Scotland today celebrates Christmas no less fully than it is kept in England, albeit unofficially; then takes her, official, New Year holiday as well and so has the best of both worlds. Nor is the celebrating done behind drawn curtains. A few years ago, driving back from Helensburgh to Milngavie in the dark on Christmas Eve, we started to count the Christmas trees in the windows of houses and flats, and had to give it up after reaching a double century less than half-way home.

# The First Gun

Our own Christmas Day always followed the same pattern.

After breakfast the family presents were given and received. This always meant one major present from father and mother combined, one lesser present from each of them, and one from grandmother. Then we went to church and after service walked along the esplanade, wishing and being wished a Merry Christmas to and by all our friends. Next, home for a very light lunch. After lunch there were presents for all the staff, indoors and out, which meant ten shillings or a pound each from father, according to length of service, a useful present from mother and grandmother, and something not useful from me. Each present was wrapped separately with its accompanying card. After that, preparations for dinner were put in hand and anyone who wanted tea, grandmother, of course, excepted, had to go to the kitchen for it and, maybe, snaffle a mince-pie and be shooed out by Mrs O'Callaghan as soon as finished. Meanwhile, mother, single-handed, would lay and decorate the dinner-table, which no one was allowed to see before dinner was announced. Father and I were putting the finishing touches to the Christmas tree in the smoking-room and hanging little, frivolous presents on it for everybody. Parcels which had arrived by post were heaped round the bottom of the tree.

As a rule there were four or five guests for dinner. Colonel Jimmy, Miss Reid, matron of the Cottage Hospital, and a bachelor Doctor Anderson who no longer practised were hardy perennials, and there were usually two or three more who might otherwise have had to spend a lonely Christmas. By seven o'clock the champagne was on ice and the wines decanted, the tree ready but not lit up; with candles, not the electricity of today, it was unsafe to light up your tree unless there was someone present to keep an eye on it. Then everyone went up to change.

The guests would arrive at 7.45. Grandmother's chair was ready in the hall, and Jimmy and Dr Anderson would go up and carry her down. There were sherry and madeira in the drawing-room, but everyone went in to dine at eight sharp. Dinner never waited upon pre-prandial drinking, the cocktail was still in the future, and gin was regarded as a cheap tipple for the working-class woman. Certainly no self-respecting Highlander would touch it when whisky was available, and when was it not?

Making all due allowances for time, a shaky memory and for nostalgia, I think we used to be a very gay and colourful lot. There was seldom a tail-coat or a dinner-jacket at table. Father wore Highland dress; kilt, grey velvet tunic, lace jabot and ruffles. So did Jimmy, Dr Anderson and I. As far as colour went, we held our own with the ladies.

The dinner was the traditional Christmas dinner preceded by oysters from Benderloch and ending with a table bestrewn with torn cracker tinsel between the silver bonbonnières, loaded with crystallised fruit and chocolates, wine glowing in cut-glass goblets under the candle-shades, and caps on every head. On this one night of the year, ladies did not leave the dining-room, but took a glass of port with the gentlemen before coffee was served in the drawing-room, while father and I went to light up the tree in a darkened library. Then there was the tree, more giving of gifts and a visit from Piper Maclean, Duggie Maclean the baker in private life, and we danced reels and strathspeys to shake down the dinner while grandmother criticised our steps from her chair in the corner. But at last the piper took his dram, a half-pint of malt whisky fifteen years old in a Jacobite goblet kept for very special occasions, and it went down his throat in one smooth, unhurried swallow (the right way to drink good whisky), and there were lesser drams for the guests and Christmas was over for another year.

On that particular Christmas morning after breakfast father had looked across the table and said:

'I forgot to tell you, but we're shooting at Dunollie on Boxing Day.'

I remembered the empty cabinet in the smoking-room.

'Hadn't I better run down to MacDougall the ironmonger and see if he has the gun?'

'I don't think that will be necessary. Suppose you have a look under the sideboard.'

And under the sideboard there was the long, flat, oblong 'boxie'. 'That's your Christmas present,' father went on. 'Your mother and I both thought it was time you had one of your own.'

Off came the brown-paper wrappings. Gift wrappings were unknown in those days. And there was a green canvas gun-case with leather-bound corners and my initials stamped on the canvas. And inside was a sixteen-bore double-barrelled hammer-gun by Cogswell and Harrison.

Father grinned at me.

'You needn't be afraid about this one. It shoots straight. I tried it at the testing-ground when I was up in town. I know hammers aren't fashionable any more, but this is a good gun from a good maker and it must last you till your twenty-first birthday when we'll see about a pair of Purdeys for you.'

A gun of my own, a gun with my initials engraved on a silver disc let into the walnut stock! And my name on the case! And suddenly there was a great wave of gratitude pouring out of me and no way of expressing it properly.

'It's . . . it's wonderful, father. She's a beauty . . . thank you both very, very much.'

'Give me time to light my pipe and we'll see if you can hit a clay pigeon with it.'

That was like father. He always understood that one must immediately use something new. I went out into the snow and hefted the gun. The stock was exactly right, so was the throw-off; she came up like a feather and nestled under my cheek as though she'd been built for me by the great James Purdey himself. It was a bad case of love at first sight. But it endured too. That old sixteen-bore killed pig and peacock in Malaya, quail and duck in Egypt; snipe, woodcock, grouse, partridge and pheasant in Scotland, pigeons and pheasants in Germany, hares in France. And I never shot better with any gun. But when the time for the Purdeys came round, I was shooting Huns with an eighteen-pounder field-piece and, after the war, there was never the same pleasure in shooting as there had been before. Today, nothing would persuade me to shoot at driven birds or slowly bring down the foresight of a rifle to a stag's shoulder. Shooting for the pot, yes, occasionally. But never shooting for shooting's sake.

# The First Millionaire

ODDLY enough, he was not American. His name was Donald Smith, son of a small shopkeeper in the small town of Forres in Morayshire. When he died in 1914 he was the Lord Strathcona and Mountroyal, a Knight Grand Cross of St Michael and St George and the Royal Victorian Order, High Commissioner for Canada and Governor of the Hudson Bay Company. In between he found time to scrawl his signature across the North American Continent in steel rails; he created the Canadian Pacific Railway. He suppressed the Red River Rebellion, he raised a regiment for the Queen's service, and did more to tighten the bonds between Canada and the Mother Country than anyone else of his time. It was a considerable achievement by any standards you care to apply.

Not long ago, when we were living in a house in Highgate Village, our nearest public library lay at the farther side of Highgate Cemetery in the Borough of St Pancras. The shortest way to it took one through the lower part of the cemetery, an interesting place in its own right, where the mortal remains of such diverse personalities as the last Marquess of Clanricarde (the miser marquess), Karl Marx, Wilkie Bard the vaudeville comedian, and Michael Faraday the scientist, rest in supposed peace. The first mausoleum on the left-hand side as you entered from Swain's Lane, a simple, well-proportioned affair, without pride of heraldry or pomp of power, in polished red granite, bore the words 'Strathcona and Mountroyal' incised over the door. Passing it, I used to bow in memory of the old gentleman who gave a small boy the first whole golden sovereign he ever owned.

Appropriately enough it was a railway, though not a trans-continental one, which introduced father to Lord Strathcona.

We came to Argyllshire when there was only the Callander and Oban Railway to link Oban with Edinburgh and Glasgow. To reach Benderloch, Appin, Creagan, Duror or Ballachulish, all small places on the shores of Loch Linnhe, one had to travel by steamer. MacBraynes, the shipowners who served the Western Isles and served them well, were monopolists and did not own ships enough for a really adequate service. So the Caledonian Railway were approached by local interests and invited to consider the building of a branch line to Ballachulish Ferry. This meant building two bridges, one at Creagan and one at the mouth of Loch Etive above the Falls of Lora. In this business, father acted as a kind of catalyst, marshalling local support, negotiating with the lairds whose land would be affected, putting the case to the railway and, eventually, supervising the draft of the Bill for Parliament.

As the owner of Glencoe, Lord Strathcona was an interested party. He had recently built himself a new house at the mouth of the Glen, high up on the hillside. It was said that he had been driven out of the original Big Hoose of Glencoe by the ghosts, which would not have surprised anyone who knew the place; but the clouds of midges which infest the flats where the Cona River runs into the loch also had something to do with his move. Although he possessed a small yacht, he preferred, when possible, to travel by train, and always by special train, an expense at which royalty boggles today. Perhaps one should here explain that the multitude of yachts which graced Oban Bay were not wholly pleasure craft. It was then very much the fashion to boast of your 'little place in the Highlands' and entertain your friends there. But some of these 'places' were very remote indeed. Some were only accessible from the sea: island estates like Rhum, Canna, Lunga, Ulva, Eigg, Coll and Colonsay to name a few.

Other shooting-lodges in Ardnamurchan, Morven and Ardgour were off the track beaten by MacBrayne paddle-wheels, which maybe only called once a week. For the owners or tenants of such places a yacht was as necessary as a car is today. Supplies had to come from Oban, the railhead; guests had to be ferried back and forth. It would have been possible to live off the country, but an unrelieved diet of grouse, salmon and venison can be just as boring as one of bully beef. Also the Edwardian palate was both sophisticated and selective.

Most tenants and some lairds regarded the autumn sojourn in the Highlands as a holiday, an escape from normal surroundings, enhanced by a variety of sport in some of the loveliest and wildest country in the world. Lord Strathcona was not of their number. Wherever he went, his work and his personal staff went with him. They travelled (by special train) from the big house in Grosvenor Square to the bigger one in Glencoe. There was quite a sensation in Argyll when it became known that there were six, *six* telephones in Glencoe to one in the Duke's castle of Inveraray. At Glencoe, office hours were kept just as they were in London. Many of his guests were diplomats and men of business like himself. In Glencoe they would find 'an executive suite' with a telephone and a very competent office staff on call if they needed such services. It followed that Glencoe house-parties were unlike any others. There were social guests and business guests and seldom the twain did meet, except round the dinner-table. The host himself was not often about till evening. Social guests, however, could not complain of neglect. Every thinkable amenity of Highland life was provided for them, and some that the Highlands had never seen before, like the rainbow trout with which a lochan in the grounds had been stocked, and the maple-trees of Canada which, alas, refused to flourish. All in all, the country was delighted with a new type of magnate who never pretended to be other than he was, and never aspired to recognition in any quarter whatever. The result was, of course, that those who expected to be wooed, themselves went a-wooing. And however unnaturally rich he was,

Lord Strathcona was, after all, a Scot and that fact gave satisfaction all round.

Every year father and mother spent a fortnight or ten days at Glencoe. Having met Lord Strathcona in Oban when the Occasion of the Whole Golden Sovereign took place, I was asked too. The sovereign business happened very simply. Hitherto, from time to time, like any other school-boy, half-sovereigns had been pressed into my hot and sticky hand by benevolent relatives and friends. But they were always snatched away by mother and put into a wretched, but very strong, metal savings-bank. What went into it never came out again. Lachie and I tried every method known to boys and burglars. We were handicapped by the fact that we daren't smash the thing with a sledge. But on this occasion Lord Strathcona himself insisted that it was mine to spend and made no restriction as to what it might be spent on. All he did say was, 'When I was your age that would have kept me for a whole month.' Gifts to boys in those days were usually accompanied by moral reflections.

For a lad of my age, Glencoe House was a bit of an ordeal at first, though I took to it as a duck to water. Never before had I been valeted by a footman or consulted whether tea or coffee should be brought to me in the morning, or whether I would prefer breakfast in bed or downstairs. Hospitable habits of the age are well reflected in the following tale. A guest arrived at a country house and was taken to his room by the footman appointed to look after him. The following dialogue ensued:

| | |
|---|---|
| FOOTMAN: | In the morning, sir . . . would you prefer tea, coffee or chocolate? |
| GUEST: | Tea, thank you; just tea. |
| FOOTMAN: | Certainly, sir. Will you have China, India or Assam? We have them all. |
| GUEST: | India . . . just an ordinary cup of tea. |
| FOOTMAN: | Yessir. And how will you take it, sir? Cream, milk or lemon, sir? |

# The First Millionaire

GUEST:     Milk, please.

FOOTMAN:   Certainly, sir. Would you prefer Jersey, Hereford
           or Ayrshire, sir?

Well, if it wasn't quite that, it wasn't very far removed from it.
Would I care to stalk? Oh, yes . . . a rifle would be available . . .
or fish? There was the loch in the grounds or the River Cona, or
a day on the hill with a keeper and the dogs . . . a drive in one of
his Lordship's cars, perhaps? The automobile had made its bow
in Argyll by then.

Father spent his time stalking. Mother took advantage of
motor transport to pay calls on friends in remote places beyond
her normal range. So, left behind, rather shy and defenceless, I
fell victim to a female. She was a duke's daughter, four times my
age, with a passion for clock-golf which she played to rules of her
own making. The principal one was that if she didn't hole out in
one, she was allowed another shot. But not me. She had a special
putter, her own invention. It had a triangular head of gunmetal,
the shaft ran into the centre of the triangle and each face had a
different loft. She putted croquetwise, left hand on top, wore a
monocle and tried to teach me Gaelic all at one and the same
time. Later it was allowed to leak out that she had brought a set of
pipes with her, so she was asked to play them after dinner and did,
marching round the table like the pipe-major of a Highland regiment, to Lord Strathcona's professed delight. The truth was she
played very badly, but because she was who she was, and might
turn up in any house one stayed at, she had to be accepted, like
some Act of God, and appeased if possible.

Two days of clock-golf passed before I plucked up courage and
appealed to Caesar. Caesar chuckled in his white beard and sent
me off to fish the Cona with a gillie. Her ladyship scared the pants
off me, or would have had I worn any.

Much as I love the Highlands, and much as I would like to live
there permanently among the glens, the bens and the brown peat
burns – almost anywhere north of Stirling would do – nothing

would ever persuade me to live in Glencoe. There is no eerier or more accursed spot in all Scotland. It is one thing to motor down the new road with the sun shining and the cloud shadows chasing each other across the flanks of the hills on either hand, but it was quite another to drive down the old road from Kingshouse after dark behind a frightened young horse, with a thunderstorm rolling round the peaks and the bleak landscape lit by lightning flashes; or, as happened later, to come down the same road with chains on the tyres through heavy snow, ghostly and soundless save for the yap-yap-yurr of a hill fox, and stopping every so often to shoo away the deer, hypnotised by the headlights, which had come down looking for food and shelter. I make no claim to being psychic, although perfectly willing to believe in any ghost that takes the trouble to become visible or audible, but there is a feeling about that well-named Glen of Weeping which induces cold fear and revulsion.

Of course, like every Highland boy, I knew the tale of the massacre, a small matter considered beside the improvements thought up by the Gestapo of all too recent years. But the thing was done by black treachery by Scots upon Scots, and it has left an indelible mark on that grim place. Perhaps that is why I so disliked the tartan worn by the duke's daughter.

But I don't suppose it ever bothered Lord Strathcona. When in residence he was seldom seen outside his own grounds. He would take the air of an evening in his customary suit of sober black, a pot hat on his head and a stick in his hand. At such times he preferred a companion who would free his mind of the day's work. On such occasions he was a wonderful companion. He never talked down to a boy but treated him as an equal. He could tell stories of trapping furs and fishing through holes cut in the ice of frozen lakes, stories of the Red River Rebellion and stories of moose killed for meat rather than sport. When father and mother were there he was apt to draw morals, because, I suppose, he thought that parents would expect him to talk that way to their offspring. After all, he himself was the success story personified. Canada was his favourite topic, Canada and the chances offered by Canada to young folk. If anyone in Glencoe wanted to emigrate, Lord Strathcona would pay their fares to any destination they asked for and see that they had enough money to live on until they found work. But if they didn't like it, they had to make their own way home. He was at great pains to make sure that both the geography and history of the Empire were properly taught in local schools. He commissioned and published school primers on Canada, Australia and New Zealand. Scots, in his opinion, made the best colonists of all, and by sending good Scots to Canada, he felt he was benefiting both those he sent and the country he sent them to.

During these walks all kinds of unlikely fauna would pop out of the wood. Count Benckendorff, the Russian Ambassador, recruiting himself with Russian cigarettes and the evening air. The Count carried diplomatic discretion to the point of total speechlessness, and very seldom uttered a word except to his host and then only in private. Ladies dreaded sitting beside him at dinner for that reason. Graf Wolff Metternich, the German Ambassador, who called me 'Red Boy', and at each encounter would solemnly shake hands and no less solemnly inquire:

'You have caught fish today, Red Boy?'

'Yes, sir.'

'Was it a large fish?'

'Not very.'

'Zo. You find satisfaction in the catching of small fishes?'

'Oh, yes, sir.'

'Ach zo. But I, I prefer to catch the large fishes.'

Then there would be a burst, an explosive burst of loud laughter, another handshake and his Excellency would walk off pondering high matters and leaving me wondering what it was all about. For the dialogue, the handshakes and the laughter were repeated every time we encountered each other, and became a private joke in the house party.

Lord Strathcona never fell into the pit dug for himself by another millionaire in the Hebrides. When Lord Leverhulme, the founder of Lever Brothers, tried to impose from above a very well-intentioned benevolence upon the islanders of Lewis and Harris, he met with implacable opposition. He started off on the wrong leg, because at the time he was raised to the peerage, newspaper gossip said that he intended to take the title of Lord of the Isles, one of the oldest and most romantic in all Scottish history. This was as strongly resented as it was untrue. The islanders called him the *bodach an shiabain* or the old soap man, and refused to co-operate for their own good so resolutely that Lord Leverhulme was compelled to give up all his plans for building up a big fishing industry, but not before he had lost two million pounds from his own pocket.

Father once came back from Stornoway chuckling over a story that illustrated the strength of island feeling. He was walking down to the pier with a local solicitor when they were passed by two smart-looking girls in their twenties. Both wore silk stockings, as rare in the islands as . . . as teetotallers. Both wore a touch of make-up on their faces, which no island girl would have dared to do. They were what they looked like, two London typists on Leverhulme's staff.

'Who are those two?' asked father.

'Ach,' hissed his companion, 'and what would they be now but two of Lord Leverhulme's whores!'

Lord Strathcona was a dyed in the wool imperialist, something which the alchemy of time has turned into a dirty word associated with the 'exploitation of coloured races'. The coloured races, for all their fanatical nationalism, are led by brains cultivated in British universities. But the solid and visible results of the Strathcona brand of imperialism, huge tracts of cultivated land surrounding splendid and prosperous cities like Ottawa, Toronto, Sydney, Wellington and Singapore, to name a few, are conveniently forgotten. Canada, Australia and New Zealand alone are good arguments for Strathcona and his like. Of course there have been policies and incidents to deplore. Even politicians are human and fallible, whatever they would have us believe. But the record stands and need call no blush to any cheek untinted, or untainted, by the red of left-wing extremism.

Our host at Glencoe had the liveliest contempt for abstainers and abstinence. He would loudly inveigh against teetotalism at his own table. He argued that anyone who allowed a craving for drink or tobacco to get out of hand was a poor creature, but that he who abstained from either amenity from fear of its getting the better of him was a coward, in his view a far, far worse thing than an addict. However much he exhorted his guests to drink deep, he himself never drank more than the half of a liqueur-glass of brandy after dinner and, perhaps, smoked one cigar a week.

Quite often he would vanish. He would be at dinner one evening and not the next. A telegram would be delivered, a special train ordered, and apologies conveyed to his guests at breakfast. He had been called to London. Had he lived today, he would have been a valued customer of Trans-Canada airlines. The year before his death he achieved his hundredth crossing of the Atlantic. The truth was, of course, that although he did all that was expected of him as an Argyllshire magnate, his heart was where he had achieved most, in Canada.

My last recollection of him was standing on the doorsteps of Glencoe House, seeing us off after a lunch-party. I had grown up quite a bit since the days when the duke's daughter had so frightened me, and Graf Wolff Metternich had been replaced by Prince Lichnowsky.

'Goodbye, Red Boy,' said Lord Strathcona, shakings hands. 'Come back soon and see if you can catch the large fishes!'

I never did.

# Shepherd's Pie and
# Baked Jam Roll

SHEPHERD'S pie always was and still is a favourite dish of my own, but I don't believe that anyone ever made it quite so appetising as did Mrs O'Callaghan; and that is a considered statement, not wishful thinking induced by nostalgia. Nor, as will be seen, was I alone in that opinion. She never minced the mutton, she cut it up in small cubes, mixed them with cubed vegetables and a sauce of her own contriving based on field mushrooms, not the tasteless, insipid, cultivated variety; she then covered the lot with mashed potato having lots of fresh butter, salt and pepper in it, and browned the pie well in a hot oven. It was good. To me, better than roast beef, roast pork or roast mutton, if only because there was never any argument about eating up the fat.

In those days you were supposed to eat everything set before you; fat was 'good for you, Donald', much as I hated it, and the clean plate ranked high among the canons of domestic discipline. In our house it was somewhat relaxed after a dreadful scene which featured Great-Uncle William and his son, James. James, a year or two my senior, had the bad luck to draw a bad egg at breakfast. It was indubitably bad, with a badness that proclaimed itself all over the dining-room. He was commanded to finish it up and refused to do so. Despite the pleas and sympathy of everyone within sniffing distance of the egg, Great-Uncle William removed James from the dining-room, beat him severely and issued orders that he should have nothing to eat until the horrid thing had been consumed. The situation was taken care of by Mrs O'Callaghan, who promptly threw out the bad egg, substituted a good one to be ceremonially eaten in the presence of Great-Uncle William, and fed James a whacking great breakfast in the kitchen as soon as Great-Uncle William was out of the house. After that there was much less of 'Eat up your nice fat, Donald'.

One summer morning mother announced that she was going to lunch with the Patten MacDougalls of Gallanach. Father, she said, would not be in for lunch next day because he had county council meetings in Oban, when he always lunched at the Station Hotel. And since there would only be two of us for tomorrow, I might, as a treat, order anything I liked for tomorrow's lunch except the salmon in the larder which would be wanted for dinner. Mother just didn't have time to speak with Mrs O'Callaghan, because Lamond the groom-coachman was even then bringing the carriage round to the door. So off she went under her violet lace parasol and I sloped round to the kitchen where, regardless of weather, I asked for a lunch of shepherd's pie and baked jam roll. With strawberry jam, of course. Mrs O'Callaghan agreed that both these things were possible, and declared that I should have them as requested. Having discharged that responsibility, I went to Glencruitten for a game of golf with Jimmy.

Next morning father went down to his meetings after breakfast, mother disappeared into the garden, and I went to play the endless, inconclusive game with Shadrach, Meshach and Abednego, the three big trout in our lochan which never rose at a fly, never looked at a worm and would come to the surface like fat carp to eat cake-crumbs. Once my friend Lachie, the poacher's son, did actually lay hand on Abed-nego by a masterly piece of tickling, but he wasn't as fast as Abed-nego's sense of self-preservation.

Tiring at last of this useless effort, I joined mother in the garden about noon, and had been with her some little time when

Maggie, in pink print and apron, came running from the house with a newly delivered note. Mother read it, took a deep breath and, but I'm not sure of this, actually said something unladylike under her breath.

'What,' she asked, 'did you order for lunch?'

'Shepherd's pie and baked jam roll, of course.'

'Of course,' said mother. 'Well, it's not your fault. Oh, I'll go in and see if Mrs O'Callaghan can do anything.'

As we went back she explained. The note was from father and said that Lord Breadalbane was coming to lunch with us and wanted to collect certain cuttings which mother had promised to Lady Breadalbane last time she and father had been at Black Mount. Now the Breadalbanes led a stately life in stately homes. Taymouth Castle, and Black Mount, their shooting lodge, had French chefs in the kitchen and liveried footmen all over the place, and mother considered that shepherd's pie was not a fitting dish to put before a marquess, and that baked jam roll was downright unseemly. But what could possibly be done in the time? She went into the kitchen.

'Mrs O'Callaghan, we're in awful trouble. The master's just sent to say that we have to give lunch to the Marquess of Breadalbane and there's . . .'

'There's nothing but shepherd's poy an' baked jam roll,' said Mrs O'Callaghan somewhat defensively. 'And it's tasty and sweet they are and fit for the King himself.'

'I don't suppose . . .' said mother tentatively.

'No, madam,' said Mrs O'C. firmly, without letting any suggestion come out of mother. 'I could nut . . . and will you be looking at the time now for the love of God!'

We looked at the kitchen clock and as we looked the front door-bell rang. It was 12.45.

'Marquesses is ut,' muttered Mrs O'Callaghan as we retreated. 'Sure t'will be iliphants nixt.'

Our guest was a small, stoutish man in a Campbell kilt with the Campbell nose, genial and pleasant as the day was long. It was rumoured throughout the county that his wife was the major partner in the marriage, although she was very careful not to let it appear so in public. They were a childless couple and lived, so it was said, under a curse. One of the Breadalbane earls, or else his countess in the absence of her lord, had caused a witch to be burned without bothering very much to look into the case for the defence. From the heart of the flames, the woman cursed the House of Breadalbane and declared that the lands and title should never pass from father to son until all their lands were lost to them. Oddly enough, that is just what happened. The marquessate died with our guest of that afternoon; the older earldom went to a cousin, and when that cousin's son, the present earl, succeeded, there were no lands left to grace the title. And a land-less lord, like a socialist peer, is to me, at any rate, a contradiction in terms.

Lord Breadalbane, nursing a dram, apologised to mother for turning up at such short notice, but his wife had insisted that he should bring back the promised cuttings for which she had caused a special bed to be prepared; and mother apologised in advance for the very simple lunch he was about to receive, explaining that the ordering thereof had been left to me and how that came about.

'Don't bother about it for a moment,' said our guest. 'Lucky to get anything at all at such short notice. Anyhow, my dear lady, I never eat a large lunch. Can't think how some fellers do it. Stuff, stuff, stuff all the time and sleep till tea. Doesn't agree with me. Never did. And all this business to discuss in the afternoon. Have to keep me wits about me. Repairs to the pier at Lismore. And that feller Maclachlan, the minister, you know. Very, very insistent. When one of these Presbyterian fellers wants something for his parish, all the others back him up. Ought to know . . . and they do know . . . we just haven't the money to please everybody. Don't expect me to eat much. Not a trencherman, never was. Mouthful of cheese. Apple. Quite enough for anybody . . . well, yes, thank you, I will. Excellent whisky this, must ask your husband where he gets it.'

And the gong went and we crossed the hall and went into the dining-room. Mother said grace, Maggie brought in the pie, put it on the sideboard, and I got up to dish it out. It smelled good, it looked good, it was good. Very good. And there were new peas from the garden to go with it. Our guest looked at his plate and sniffed.

'Nothin' like the old dishes. Nothin' I like better than a good shepherd's pie. Me wife never gives it to me.'

The Breadalbane chef, confronted by a request for shepherd's pie, would probably have either exploded or resigned on the spot.

At first all this voluble appreciation was taken as the politeness of an unexpected guest to an unprepared hostess. But it soon became apparent that the marquess meant what he said. He forgot all about his avowals of lunchtime asceticism, his substantial helping vanished like snow on the Sahara, and before I had dealt with my own plateful, I was replenishing his.

'Remarkable! Excellent cook you must have. Just the kind of thing I never can get at home. Must speak to Lady Breadalbane about it.'

Mother wore an expression I knew very well. She was on the verge of the giggles, and when I asked her to have some more, she wouldn't trust herself to speak, but just shook her head. His Lordship gobbled and gobbled and gobbled till his plate was empty again and Maggie bore out the remains of the pie, watched, I thought, a trifle wistfully by our guest. He refused claret, our normal lunchtime tipple, but refilled his glass from the whisky decanter.

But the success of the pie was a small thing compared with the acclamation that greeted the baked jam roll. It was brown and crisp without, white and light within, and liberally stained with the rich red of our home-made strawberry jam. It was always one of Mrs O'Callaghan's *chef d'œuvres*, and it seems to me that the man who can't appreciate a good baked jam roll deserves to live upon snails for the rest of his days.

Lord Breadalbane fell upon it with whoops of delight, and if the expression appears too strong for you, I have no intention of altering it. You wouldn't think that marquesses with great castles and swarms of servants need want a good jam roll. But so it happened. To him it was manna in the wilderness and corn in Egypt all rolled into one. Completely forgotten were those remarks about apples and mouthfuls of cheese. He tucked in and disposed of three slices to my two and mother's one. Then there were cheeses, fruit, port and coffee in the usual way. These, coffee excepted, he refused, which was not surprising. We went back to the drawing-room for coffee.

Lord Breadalbane lay back in a corner of the sofa. A German might have called him *aufgeblasen*, certainly he had swollen visibly.

'Wonderful lunch,' he said. 'Must tell my wife about it. Perhaps I might bring her here one day . . . or would that be askin' too much?' Mother of course said that it would be delightful if Lady Breadalbane came next time, and that she would promise to have shepherd's pie and baked jam roll, provided due notice was given, after any meeting of the county council, and, Donald, please see if Lord Breadalbane would like one of your father's cigars, the silver box on the study table. Coffee drunk, cigar pierced and lit, he went off to the garden with mother for the cuttings, and by the time they came back Lamond had harnessed the horses and brought the carriage round to carry him down to the afternoon meeting. He departed full of professed gratitude, rather red in the face and, I think, quite glad not to walk down to town.

We waved him good-bye. 'Who would have thought,' said mother, parodying Shakespeare, 'that the little man had so much room in him?' Then she laughed and said, 'I think you'd better order all the meals for really important guests; you seem to know what they like.'

When told how successful the lunch had been Mrs O'Callaghan said the last word.

'And didn't I know it? When what came back from the table wouldn't have filled the belly of a flea. Wasn't I afther tellin' you, ma'am, t'would be fit for a king, no less? And don't you be forgettin' now that all men is small boys when it comes to the stomach, marquesses or no marquesses.'

# Matters Medical

THERE was once a Member of Parliament, a rich and distinguished Highlander, well known and well liked everywhere north of Stirling. When past the middle age, he began to suffer badly from a form of dermatitis. He resented it acutely because the irritation set up prevented his sleeping properly and his work suffered accordingly. His London doctor sent him to eminent Harley Street specialists and he did what they told him to do. He was sent to the Riviera, he spent his holidays at continental spas, he had elaborate, and costly, electrical treatments and therapy by rays of different kinds. Although, from time to time, there was some alleviation, no real cure was effected. Not unnaturally he worried and began to lose faith in the whole medical profession. His malady had cost him hundreds of guineas and his sleeplessness had reached the point where he had occasionally to use morphine when a good night's sleep became absolutely necessary. One autumn, after the House had risen, he suddenly scrapped his plans for a visit to Aix and bethought him of the peace and beauty to be found in the Hebrides. There, surely he thought, a man might find rest and sleep.

The island he chose was a small one; the nearest doctor lived on its neighbour across a short arm of the sea and only came across when sent for, which was seldom.

Sir Murdoch took two rooms in the presbytery of the local priest and was looked after by his housekeeper. At first all was as well as he could have wished, but later the old, loathed irritation returned, and with it came depression and something not far removed from despair. And he had no morphine with him. He had deliberately left it behind. After some consecutive nights of sleeplessness, he made inquiries about the doctor, and learned that he was away, but that his place had been taken by a locum tenens from Oban. Eventually he wrote a note to the locum, explained his need, and enclosed his authority to procure morphine, which was signed by a name of great eminence in the profession.

When his note brought not morphine but the locum in person he was not at all pleased. He was beginning to think of the entire profession as a collection of fee-snatching bandits, and his fear was that the man might be some new-fledged youngster from Glasgow or Edinburgh, and there were very few in Scotland who did not know him by reputation as a plutocrat.

Somewhat to his surprise, the doctor turned out to be a man of his own age, tall, white-whiskered, with very blue eyes, a great crag of a nose and a manner that very clearly spelt no nonsense.

'Up to bed with you, Sir Murdoch, and into your pyjamas,' was the first command, and the MP, not a little to his own surprise, found himself doing just what he was told. The doctor came upstairs and examined him.

'Sir Clavering Bodysnatch, you'll have heard of him,' said Sir Murdoch, 'says that the trouble is . . .' and there followed a good deal of secondhand diagnosis.

'Button up,' said the doctor. 'Now listen to me. You have the itch. I'll send across a pot o' sulphur ointment by McInnes the ferryman. Rub it in tonight, all over. Do it thoroughly. The same thing tomorrow and I'll be back to see you the day after. And there'll be nae morphine for you, ma mannie.'

Sir Murdoch protested, but the only satisfaction he got was the sight of the doctor tearing up his permit to buy morphia. Having done so, he went away. That afternoon the ointment came and the patient followed his instructions. He got some sleep that night. After the second application he slept really well. The doctor called again. 'Just keep on with the ointment,' he said. 'You'll be fine in a week.' And it was even so. Sir Murdoch could hardly believe what had happened. A request for the doctor to call again was met with blank refusal. 'You don't need me. Others do.' Sir Murdoch changed his tactics and tried the social approach . . . would the doctor give him the pleasure of his company at dinner? He came and the M.P. tried to word his gratitude, but was brushed aside while the priest and the doctor discussed the mediaeval problem about how many angels could be expected to dance on the point of a needle. As he was leaving, Sir Murdoch mentioned the matter of his fee and hinted that he would be prepared to pay handsomely for such services. He got his account on the following day. He was charged ten shillings for two visits, and two shillings for the pot of ointment, which was a very large one indeed.

The hero of that episode was Doctor Robert MacKelvie, who brought me into this world, stood godfather to me, and was almost as much a part of the home establishment as Mrs O'Callaghan herself. For then the doctor was considered art and part of the family life, a close, familiar friend to the whole household. Paradoxically, his services were less in general request, and he was not called in unless he was really needed. We used fewer drugs and those less frequently than people do today. Pep pills, tranquillisers, stabilisers, vitamin pills simply were not, and we got along pretty well without them. For instance, as a lad, I cannot recall having ever seen a bottle of aspirin tablets in the house. That might be a tribute to the quality of father's whisky or our own constitutions, but we never used them. Mother kept some nasty things called *cachets fièvres* which she procured from Paris and were regarded as sovereign in the event of bad headaches or unexpected temperatures. They were about the size of a shilling and constructed of something like cardboard made from rice paper. An adult could just swallow one with water, but they would stick in the adolescent throat and break there, leaving a foul aftertaste which lingered for days. They were feared and dreaded. Beside them in the domestic medicine cupboard you would find Gregory's Powder, an evil-tasting stuff administered in a spoonful of jam and therefore preferred to the licorice powder which, though milder, was stirred up in water and swallowed with grimaces. Other standbys were an iron tonic which blackened the teeth, quinine for colds, senna pods, mildest of the laxatives, calamine for sunburn, vaseline, lanoline, boric powder, and Mr Elliman's horse embrocation for sprains or strains. Cuts, bruises and gravel in the knees, frequent occurrences among small boys, were treated with warm water and carbolic and lanoline on lint. As a prophylactic against the common cold, a good dose of whisky, lemon, sugar and boiling water would be administered from the age of ten onwards. Nor was it thought other than normal. From the predominance of laxatives, it may be rightly inferred that we ate far more than is generally eaten today. I had more at lunch then than I eat in the whole day now. Breakfast consisted of porridge, fish and a third dish; lunch was of four courses and there were five at dinner, and that makes no allowance for afternoon tea which was then a serious matter.

But the inevitable advent of measles, mumps, scarlet fever and any sign of a temperature over a hundred degrees meant Doctor MacKelvie and none other. Having brought me into the world, he had also accepted the responsibilities of god-fatherhood and fulfilled them scrupulously in the important matter of tips, Christmas and birthday presents.

During the week his dress was rigidly professional. He wore either a morning coat or a frock coat but without silk facings; elaborately embroidered waistcoats of brocade or satin; striped trousers and a kind of hat you no longer see, a tall, black felt shaped like a topper but slightly domed at the top. I remember finding a German Professor in one of 'Elizabeth's' novels who came to stay at some Schloss for an August week without, apparently, any luggage at all. When asked what had happened to it, he replied (I quote from memory) something to this effect: "Frau Gräfin, the apparel suitable to the night I wear below the apparel appropriate to the day, and my sponge, damp and cool, is embedded in the crown of my hat".' Doctor MacKelvie's hat was instantly suggested by the Professor's speech. It would have made a splendid sponge carrier. He was a bonny fighter and it was that quality in him which signed and sealed my father's friendship with him. Together they helped to create a local Cottage Hospital which had been a crying need for many years. And in the teeth of much opposition. But above all else, he was a first-class doctor, which was why we were his patients, although, had we stuck to the rules, we should never have gone to him at all.

It is strange, but true, that in those times doctors were chosen no less for their religious convictions than for their medical skill. For the Wee Frees, a Wee Free doctor; for the Congregationalists a Congregationalist, and no Roman Catholic would think of using a heretic. So we, who were Episcopalians, ought to have had the Episcopalian doctor. Our failure to conform was resented. By the Episcopalian doctor, that is. The medical profession were well aware that each congregation was a source of patients, and if a new doctor set up in practice the first question asked would be, 'Whom does he sit under?' meaning what place of worship did he attend. Politic medicos therefore took as prominent a part in Church life as they were able to attain, and all the well-established were elders, church-wardens or lay office-bearers of one kind or another. To that rule Doctor MacKelvie was a prominent exception. He was never 'attached' to any specific religious body because his hobby was theology. He was a confirmed sermon taster who flitted from preacher to preacher, regardless of sect, and the more abstruse and intricate the preacher, the better pleased was he. From members of other professions he expected standards as high as his own. He was often disappointed. During diocesan conferences, when we kept open house for parsons from the outlying parishes of a widespread see, my father took a perverse delight in having Doctor MacKelvie to dine with them and setting the medical cat among the clerical pigeons. For most of the clergy were better versed in good works than those of St Augustine, St Thomas Aquinas or the early fathers of the Christian Church. To the doctor they were as familiar as the insides of his black bag. Nothing delighted him more than a worthy opponent. Few Scots – let's face it, a polemical race – enjoyed an argument better than he. He could argue both sides of a question equally well, and when the dust had settled could show a vanquished opponent just where his case had gone off the rails.

A good fisherman, especially with the wet fly, and a fair shot, he would come out with father and me whenever he had a week-end free. It was not often, and even on such occasions he was seldom with us at the end of the day. Some panting messenger would appear out of the blue, the doctor would take down his rod, go back to the farm where the horses were stabled, harness up and be away. To the end of his days he never refused a call, and only three in five would bring him any profit. To the truly poor, and he knew the circumstances of every family in the place, the matter of fees was never raised. Sometimes his fees brought him embarrassment, as when a Mull crofter whose wife had been saved in the Cottage Hospital rewarded her saviour with a bull calf, alive and kicking vigorously, not an easy creature to dispose of in a house in a square without any garden at all. A fair proportion of his rewards came in kind. Herrings from the fisher-folk, butter, eggs and meal with kebbuck cheese from farm and croft, the half of a fish or a brace of pheasants from the poaching fraternity. Opposite his house in Argyll Square there was a pub much frequented by drovers during the cattle sales. There was a lot of whisky taken on such festive occasions, and sometimes offence, when fighting would start. Doctor MacKelvie almost put an end to that off his own bat. One night when a row was in full swing, he, and he was well past sixty at the time, strode out of his house, crossed the square, picked up each of two combatants in turn and dropped them both in the cattle trough. After that there was less brawling under his windows.

There was an old reprobate of a fisherman who was forced by fate and economics to spend the evening of his days under his married daughter's roof. She was an excellent woman, but in her youth her sire's behaviour had been such as to make a rabid, positive, blue-ribbon teetotaller out of her. As long as the old man could get about and have his dram occasionally, he managed well enough. But when he became bedridden his discomfiture was absolute. Spirits never entered into that house in any circumstances. The old man's misery touched his doctor's heart. He had not long to live anyhow. So a tonic was prescribed. It came from the surgery in large bottles, properly corked and sealed with red wax, labelled with an official label with instructions to administer the dose, two tablespoonfuls without water, three times daily. The daughter could hardly have failed to know what the true character of the golden tonic was, but she never dared to disobey Doctor MacKelvie's instructions. The tonic was regularly administered, and supplied, till the old man slipped quietly away.

Only a few years ago I was reminded of Robert MacKelvie in rather a curious way. There was a very old Scots doctor living in Highgate, long retired. He was well past ninety when I met him. The last time we talked together, he told me that he had acted as locum for Doctor MacKelvie on several occasions. He himself came from a crofting family on the Isle of Mull. Shortly after that meeting his mind began to fail and he fell into a second childhood. In that state he forgot the English he had spoken for the greater part of his life and reverted to his native Gaelic. None of his children or grandchildren had any Gaelic of any kind, so communications within the house became difficult till a Gaelic-speaking nurse from the Hebrides was procured to look after him.

Doctor MacKelvie's rival, the Episcopalian doctor, was also his antithesis. He regarded himself as the self-appointed doctor to the nobility and gentry. He skimmed the cream of the tourist trade in the more expensive hotels, and there were many well-to-do, invalid old ladies who were charmed with his attentiveness. He impressed one and all by his reading of the second lesson on Sundays. He read well, if rather plummily, and strongly resembled the Pekinese dogs he kept. His fatal flaw was neatly described by his own daughter, then six years of age, who said that her daddy was a dear daddy but very 'pomptious'. And retribution was even then lying in wait for him. It happened on an Easter Sunday in church. Our Easter services were distinctly high church. It may have been a reaction to the Presbyterian austerity that surrounded them. On occasion one was aware of incense, which infuriated the low church verger, Mr Benwell, who would hiss into my mother's ear, 'Another sstep towards the Ssscarlet Woman!' as we went in through the porch. At Easter, all the stops were pulled out, and what with copes and mitres and stoles and chasubles and altarcloths and candles and the floral decorations provided by the devout, it was a show – and those with low church tendencies could hardly contain themselves to see How Far they would Go.

On this Sunday, the bishop was to preach and the dean took the service. The doctor read both lessons as his Easter treat. When the bishop was climbing the pulpit steps, he had the misfortune to slip and fall heavily, hitting his forehead on the edge of a step. He slid to the bottom of the steps in a crumpled heap and lay there, groaning audibly. His wife jumped to her feet and went, straight as an arrow from the bow, to his assistance. For some unknown reason the doctor considered this unseemly. Hooded and surpliced he strode to the chancel steps, held up his hand and said, 'Back, woman!' The bishop's wife was not to be deterred by mere proprieties. While the elder choristers were carrying the poor bishop through the vestry door, she brushed past the doctor with a short, muttered phrase and went to her husband's side. The doctor was left, mouth open and hand in air, looking very foolish on the chancel steps in full view of the whole congregation.

Just what the bishop's wife said to the doctor was a fruitful subject for speculation round the tea-tables for weeks to come. When at last somebody had the courage to ask her, she smiled and, with a twinkle, admitted that she had 'forgotten where she was for a moment'. The doctor's 'pomptiousness' never was quite the same again.

There was an old naval pensioner in Oban who had his own yardstick for popularity. He lived in a cottage on the Pennyfuir road and all the funerals passed his windows on their way to the Pennyfuir cemetery.

'Aye, a fery good lady she was, that one. Aye . . . and her with fifteen carritches and fifty yard o' mourners to her funeral.'

Doctor MacKelvie's funeral, it was said – I was not in Oban at the time – would have astounded old Duncan had he not previously taken the road he had watched so carefully. Nearly a quarter of the population and every 'carritch' in the place followed him to Pennyfuir, and if it is true that we survive only in the memories of those who have known us on this earth, he has survived longer than most, for no one who knew him could possibly have forgotten him.

If the doctor was a family friend, the same could not be said for the dentist. That may be postulated without detracting one jot or one tittle from either the worth or the social status of the dental profession. It just happened that we had no resident dentists in Oban then. We were served by two itinerants, one from Glasgow and the other from Edinburgh, and some of the local doctors were quite prepared to take out a tooth in emergency. It is quite wrong to associate dentistry with emergency, but, as a family, few of us ever submitted to the dentists' chair in anything less. Most of us had our dentists in Glasgow or Edinburgh and combined a visit with a week-end in the big city and an evening at the play.

I never had occasion to visit either itinerant. Mrs O'Callaghan was less fortunate. One July she displayed a face twice its normal size, wrapped round with a red bandana handkerchief filled with hot salt. This palliative was commended to her by Father MacDonald, her spiritual adviser. Here again we have the medico-clerical association but in reverse. Mother, who was as much hurt by another's pain as by any she actually suffered herself, immediately insisted upon a visit to the dentist. The Glasgow itinerant was available that day. In vain Mrs O'Callaghan protested that it was but a small trouble, and one that would be 'passin'' away av itsilf widout anny help from man'. Mother was firm. An appointment was made, and a cab ordered to bring back the sufferer after treatment in case the hill prove too much for her. She came back a good deal later than we expected, and was sent straight to bed where she remained all the following day. Mother it was who extracted the full story from her, not without difficulty, for her speech was barely intelligible.

Once inside the surgery, the array of steel instruments, the sinister drill and the gas cylinders struck terror in her heart, and she vowed that if she ever got out, 'and himsilf, the wee fella a black protestant . . . beggin' your pardon ma'am', no power on earth would ever bring her back again. So she hit on a remarkable expedient. She had every tooth in her head extracted at one single session. They were possibly in bad condition, I don't know, but anyhow the wee fella went to work and cleaned her up. For a month or so her natural volubility was diminished, but when her gums had healed, father told her she must go back to have casts for dentures prepared. There was an appalling fuss. Never, never, never again would she enter that torture-chamber. In the event, father himself had to take a morning off, conduct her personally to the dentist and stay there till the business was over and done with. He, of course, and I think the custom was general, made himself personally responsible for the fees incurred for any medical or dental treatment needed by anyone in the house. When the dentures were finally delivered they were a great success. At first she would only use her 'gnashers', as she called them, for meals. They lived in a heart-shaped casket of violet plush on the kitchen mantelpiece, below a highly coloured oleo of the martyrdom of Saint Sebastian. Later, in the interests of clear speech, she was persuaded to wear them all the time. Father, faced with a bill for guineas where he had anticipated shillings, was philosophical about it. 'What,' he asked, 'was a mouthful of teeth between friends?'

Our next emergency occurred on the other side of Scotland when we were staying with grandfather, and this time mother was the victim. She was in considerable pain and the nearest dentist was at Montrose, some ten miles away. She felt that she could not face the shaking and jolting of a train journey to Glasgow, so Montrose was decided upon. There were two dentists in the town and by an odd chance only one name between them, albeit differently spelled, Mackie and MacKay . . . but those were not the actual names. Grandfather was very insistent about choosing the right one because the other had a reputation for drinking. 'Feller puffs whisky in your face,' said grandfather, who rightly disliked whisky at second hand. This harangue was at mother's address, so I paid little attention at the time. Then he blew up over the Dogger Bank incident and delivered a piece of his mind to the absent Russian Admiral Rodjesvensky, whom grandfather always called 'Rottenstinky', and I thought it was a splendid name for an admiral who fired at fishing-smacks.

It was arranged that we should be driven to Montrose early next morning, and the boot-boy was sent into Fettercairn with a wire asking for an emergency appointment. My part was to go with mother, see her to the dentist and then 'practise at my goff' – grandfather always called it 'goff' – on the links. Golf, at that time, was almost being forced down my throat by reason of an inconsistency in grandfather. There was an exception to his anti-episcopal rule in the person of Dr Winnington Ingram, then Bishop of London. As the bishop had taken to spending his holidays at Edzell, where there was an excellent golf-course, grandfather decided that I should represent the family and play golf with the bishop whenever he wanted a game. I was therefore encouraged to practise on every possible occasion, and given five bob any time I could beat him. Not that much encouragement was ever needed to make me play golf. Just when we were nearing Montrose, mother asked, 'Can you remember which of the dentists grandfather said I was to go to?' I could not.

'Oh, well,' sighed mother, 'he'll have a telegram anyhow. I expect it will be all right.'

The horse and trap were put up at the hotel where we were to lunch, and from the porter we got the addresses of both dentists and set forth to find the nearest. It was rather a dismal-looking place in a sordid street. Mother rang the bell. She had not taken her hand from the bell pull when the door opened.

'I think,' she said, 'I had an appointment with . . .'

'Come awa' ben, madam,' was the instant reply. 'We're a' ready for ye.'

She was whisked inside in no time at all. The door banged and in that instant it did seem that there might have been a rather whiskified smell on the air, but I turned away and headed for the links. Mother was waiting for me at the hotel at lunch-time. She was in a very bad temper.

'That miserable creature!'

'Why? Did he hurt?'

'No, it wasn't that. He did nothing . . . nothing at all . . . and he had been drinking. Grandfather was perfectly right.'

'What happened?'

'He had a look and said it must come out. Then he gave me gas. And when I came out of the gas, there he was with the forceps in his hand dancing about and moaning, "Oh, I forgot the gag. Aye . . . I forgot the gag".'

'What's that?'

'You know, the rubber thing they put in your mouth to keep it open. That was enough for me. We'll go to the other one after lunch.'

Mother's sheer anger improved her spirits, and she was quite cheerful during our meal. And the other Mr MacKay turned out to be the right Mr MacKay with whom the appointment had been made, and there was no nonsense, or whisky either, about him. I waited in his waiting-room with the bound volumes of 'Punch' and the bronze knights in armour who flourished long lances on either side of the black marble clock.

After tea in the hotel we started back. Half-way home mother said, 'Donald . . . we won't tell grandfather what happened. It'll only upset him . . . and he'd never let me forget about it.'

'All right,' I told her, 'but on one condition.'

'Condition? You young ruffian! Are you going to blackmail your own mother?'

'No.'

'Then what is it?'

'That I'm allowed to drive the trap from Laurencekirk to Fettercairn.'

And I was. Nor did grandfather ever hear the truth about that expedition.

# The Eccentrics

WHEREVER you have people living far apart from one another in a sparsely populated county, especially people of small private means, you are sure to find a crop of introverts who are prone to fall over into eccentricity.

Argyllshire, where all these conditions were present, was no exception, so three are now presented for your examination.

First, Maclaine of Lochbuie. Not, by the way, The Maclaine of Lochbuie. There is an old saying on this subject. In Scotland we have but three 'Thes': The Chisholm, the Pope and the Devil. MacNeill of MacNeill, Mackintosh of Mackintosh, yes. But not The MacNeill or The Mackintosh.

There are two main branches of Clan Maclean – Duart and Lochbuie – and from these two all minor branches of the clan, such as Ardgour and Pennycross, are descended. Some eight hundred years ago two brothers, originally from Ireland, who had acquired vast estates in Argyllshire and elsewhere, built for themselves castles in the Isle of Mull – one at Duart and the other at Lochbuie. It cannot positively be ascertained which was the elder brother, but in recent years, after much bickering, the chieftainship has been finally invested in Maclean of Duart.

The men of Lochbuie, nevertheless, have a record to be proud of, one of total loyalty to the Royal House of Stuart. They fought with Montrose, they fought with Claverhouse and they fought with Charles Edward Stuart and quit them like men. Their loyalty brought them nothing but loss of blood and treasure at a time when the surrounding Campbells, who adhered to the House of Hanover, flourished like green bay-trees.

The Lochbuie of my youth was very well liked by everyone except his bankers. Cheerfully, habitually and chronically he overspent his income and mortgaged his land. He liked of all things to 'cut a dash', in the Edwardian phrase. We West Highlanders are vain men. Every so often he would pack his full Highland evening-dress with his gold-hilted dirk and gold buckles, his Valenciennes lace jabot and ruffles, his diamond brooches and velvet tunic, put a brace of eagle's feathers in the gold clasp of his bonnet and fare south to London, just to show the Sassenach what a Highland Chief ought to look like. And he was a very handsome, well-built man. By night he was a Raeburn come to life. He could talk with perfect truth of his castle, his moors and his vassals (or tenants), for at the time he possessed all these things. What he didn't tell the Sassenach was that his moors produced few grouse, his stags were few and far between, and parts of his castle barely kept out the weather. And his tenants looked very warily at him. For which there was good reason. In his younger days he had a certain tenant who would not pay his rent. In an island like Mull almost everybody knows everybody else's business with uncanny accuracy. It was well known that the defaulter could well afford to pay. He just preferred not to. One night, Lochbuie and two of his gillies called on the defaulter. It was a dark, cold night. They rousted him out of bed and tied him up carefully so that he should come to no harm, took him out on Lochbuie in a rowing-boat, dropped him overboard and towed him through the dark and icy water till he agreed to pay. It did not take long. A bit drastic, you may think, but the sympathy of the men of Mull was with Lochbuie. Was he not ready with the restorative dram when the drookit creature was brought ashore, and had he not ordered hot blankets to be prepared against his tenant's return? As it was, the matter never came to court, nobody mentioned the word 'damages' and thereafter the Lochbuie tenants paid punctually, even if they did not pay much.

His participation in the London season was part pleasure – the greater part – and part business. He sang the praises of his own land and did what he might to find a tenant for the shooting season and so save an agent's commission. When he first met the Princess Radziwill, he thought he had found just the person he was looking for. The Princess was as mighty a huntress as the fabled Diana. She had shot practically everything from the elephant downwards. She was rich beyond the dreams of avarice, and the handsome Lochbuie made an excellent impression. But, alas, the Highlands had nothing new to offer her. She had already grassed a Royal of sixteen points at Applecross and shooting grouse no longer interested her. It was then that a brilliant idea struck Lochbuie. He invited her to stay with him in the autumn and bag one of the very rare, almost extinct, mountain goats which could only be found on the mountains of Mull. That she had never heard of this creature was not altogether surprising. Nobody else had. But the suggestion of something new to shoot had its effect, and by the time Lochbuie had finished talking, Ovis Poli had nothing on the mountain goats of Ben More. The conversation lingered in the Princess's mind.

He had long forgotten both goats and Princess when her telegram arrived that September. She would like very much, if Lochbuie's invitation still held, to come for the second week of the month and try to bag a mountain goat. He promptly telegraphed a warm welcome by return and looked about him for a goat to sacrifice. He bought three.

Once set on a given course, Lochbuie could be very ingenious. He thought out his campaign and made preparations which included a trip across the Sound to Oban, a very private interview with a taxidermist and the redecoration of the castle's state bedroom. Robert the Bruce had slept there. Elizabeth I could never have got there alive.

In due course the Princess arrived at Lochbuie. Pipers marched before her from the pier to the castle. Her host and his son, whom we shall meet later, escorted her through great, draughty stone halls bedecked with displays of ancient weapons, targes and stags' heads. Serving-men in kilts abounded on every hand, and if some of them smelt of the byre rather than the servants' hall, perhaps she wouldn't notice it. Lochbuie, of course, had no longer any thought of a let. He had involved himself in a situation and meant to see it through. He was now solely concerned with the entertainment of a very distinguished guest in a manner of which his forefathers would have approved. A wild goat she wanted, and if there were no wild goats, well, she should have a goat.

The stalk took place on the very next day. It was prolonged and arduous. There was much considering of prevailing winds, much creeping through heather and bog-myrtle and crawling 'thorough bush, thorough briar'. There was even a bit of rock-climbing before the creature was 'spied' on a rocky plateau on the farther side of a corrie. The Princess lived up to her high reputation. The wild mountain goat fell at the first shot, but when they had scrambled down one side of the corrie and up the other, it had vanished. Then Lochbuie himself saw it. It had fallen over the edge of a cliff and lay on the rocks below.

The goat would be brought to the castle in the evening, and meanwhile there would be lunch and another stalk in the afternoon if the Princess felt so inclined. No sooner had the party moved away than a gillie who had been instructed to throw the beast over the cliff came out of the cave in which he had been hiding and bore away the quarry. But the Princess was no glutton. Not for her to slay another specimen of a rapidly disappearing species. She had her wild goat. One would be enough. Lochbuie thought of the money he had wasted on the three when one would have done. But he couldn't think of everything. To do him justice he had not forgotten much.

That evening he was full of apologies. His orders had been misunderstood, and if nobody had been hanged for his carelessness, that was the fault of the degenerate age we lived in. The head, by far the finest ever seen in Mull, had been sent over to Oban on the afternoon boat. It would be set up and duly forwarded to her with Lochbuie's compliments. And so it was.

What the taxidermist did to that ancient billy was quite beyond belief. This came to me at second hand from one of the taxidermist's daughters, then, in my eyes, and not in mine alone, the most delectable of Oban's daughters. The horns were taken out of the skull and those of some obscure African antelope put in in their place. The beard and hair in the cheeks were dyed brownish red. Green glass eyes went into the eye-sockets, and poor old billy was so tarted up when they had done with him that his own mother would have fled from him in terror. All he lacked was a rhinoceros horn between his eyes. The reconstituted billy was duly dispatched to Princess Radziwill, and duly acknowledged as a rare and precious addition to her collection of trophies. It would always remind her of the wonderful day she had spent at Lochbuie. If it was still there when the Russians occupied the Radziwill country seat in Poland two wars later, old billy must have given their zoologists most furiously to think.

Sir Duncan Campbell of Barcaldine was about as different a kind of man from Lochbuie as anyone could possibly imagine. He was much older, he was a bachelor, an ascetic, an historian, a genealogist, a recluse and a Herald – Rothesay Herald, if memory doesn't betray me. He lived alone in his ancient family seat of Barcaldine Castle on the shores of Loch Linnhe near Benderloch, and shunned the social life altogether. Although men are for the most part happy enough to leave a fellow creature alone, once he has made it clear that he prefers to live that way, their wives feel differently. Women regard a solitary, bookful life as a probable mask for secret and vicious debauchery. To them it was very wrong that Sir Duncan, the last baronet of Barcaldine, should be unmarried, and that a perfectly good hereditary title, in a county where titles did not grow on every bush, should lapse from want of enterprise on his side. There was no want of it on theirs. By degrees their husbands dissuaded them from sending invitations to

Barcaldine, or even from leaving cards there – a good excuse for peering through the windows. For sport in any form Sir Duncan gave not a damn.

Eventually he established a *status quo* which satisfied him. He was practically forgotten, and his front door bell never rang except when he received a visit from some learned colleague. So absorbed in the past was he that had the Loch Ness Monster escaped into Loch Linnhe and stood on its tail outside the bailey of Barcaldine, Sir Duncan would not have bothered to cross the room to look. But if you wanted to know why Callum Campbell of Lochow, who died in 1324, bore the arms of Lochow undifferenced despite his undoubted bastardy, why then, Sir Duncan was your man.

So when in the autumn of 1909 two of his neighbours, Sir Charles Stuart of Achara and MacAlpine Downie of Appin, both of them Stuarts by blood, received invitations to a stag dinner-party at Barcaldine, their respective womenfolk were much too intrigued to let them refuse. Sir Duncan's letters said that he had a problem on his mind which concerned them all, and that he would be grateful for their guidance and advice. The invitation did not include their ladies, who indulged in delightful visions of their lords eating burned mutton off wooden platters served by a hairy, half-naked Campbell gillie.

They would have been disappointed by the reality. Sir Duncan turned out to be a charming host whose wine, table and service left nothing to be desired. Then, over the claret – Sir Duncan disapproved of port as an English innovation – he posed his problem.

Here one must interrupt him to point out that this was the year 1909, the year of the famous People's Budget. A Welshman called Lloyd George had become Chancellor of the Exchequer. That he was the most dangerous and inflammatory phenomenon to come out of Wales since Henry Tudor overthrew the Plantagenets in 1485 was generally agreed. He had launched an attack on the very bedrock of the British Constitution, the Landed Interest. He had dared to tax them and promised to tax them yet more heavily. The Tory world was furious, far, far beyond the usual asperity of political exchange. The Tory Press had called Mr Lloyd George a liar, a thief, a mountebank, a Communist, an Anarchist, a dangerous demagogue, a fomenter of revolution, a bravo, a traitor, a devil's advocate, a Socialist wolf in Liberal clothing, and a Welsh poacher. His Grace the Duke of Beaufort had openly expressed his desire to see 'Lloyd George and Winston Churchill in the middle of twenty couple of dog hounds'. If land taxes were bad for the great landowners, the Cavendishes and Russells, the Sutherlands and the Buccleuchs, they were a far more serious menace to the small landowner who could just 'get by' without them. The Welsh Wizard loomed dangerously over a county which, normally, was little interested in politics and rather given to despise the politician.

Sir Duncan began to explain something rather abstruse out of Scottish history. How in the old days before the Union of England and Scotland in 1603, each Chief had the right of pit and gallows, of the High Justice, the Middle and the Low, and just how and when they had signed away those rights and surrendered all judiciary rights to the Crown. Sir Charles, a prosperous London solicitor, nodded knowledgeably; MacAlpine Downie wondered what the old boy was driving at.

It had chanced, Sir Duncan continued, that at the time in question, Barcaldine was the property of a female infant three years old. The Castle was vacant, the owner in Cornwall. Consequently no Campbell of Barcaldine had ever, *in propria persona*, signed away the rights he had referred to. He himself, he said, was a Tory in spite of his clan's Whiggish associations. He was aware that the general feeling in the county must be Liberal. At any rate they voted Liberal. But this Land Tax was something that went deeper than party politics. It threatened the very structure of society. Achara and Appin nodded. They were landowners themselves. Now it had occurred to Barcaldine, that if a Liberal rally could be arranged in the county and Lloyd George invited to address it . . . it might not be impossible to bring the man to Barcaldine.

'But why?' asked Achara. 'What good would that do?'

'Oh,' said Sir Duncan, 'I could have him hanged . . . over the gate there. I still have a couple of men here who would do whatever I told them.'

There would be a considerable fuss. He realised that. But there would also be an interesting case to be argued. Achara would know more about that than he did, and even if he lost and had to hang in his turn, well, he was an old man without much to look forward to, and the rest of his life was nothing compared with the good of the country as a whole.

His guests sat dumbfounded. The host undoubtedly meant what he said. Appin said afterwards that it sounded so *blasted* reasonable. Perhaps he was hypnotised by his surroundings, in which nothing had changed much for three hundred years. They dined off an old refectory table lit by candles in silver sconces, a log fire blazed on the open stone hearth, and the stone floor was covered with deerskin rugs. Their very clothes had hardly changed in that time. It did not seem the least preposterous that three gentlemen over their wine should be plotting to murder the Chancellor of the Exchequer.

Achara broke the silence. 'No, Barcaldine,' he said. 'It just wouldn't do. It would be too gross a breach of hospitality, to put it no higher than that.'

Barcaldine nodded. 'I was afraid you might say that. But mind you, I'm quite prepared to bear the brunt of the odium, if any odium were incurred. I had no intention of making accomplices of you. I wanted the opinions of two men who are more in touch with the world of today than I am.'

Achara saw the light. 'But, Barcaldine, that is just what you have done. In law, Appin and I are already your accomplices before the fact. If you were to take any active steps, we'd have to go to the police to save our skins.'

Barcaldine shook his head. 'I must take your word for it, Sir Charles . . . but it's a pity. Aye, a great pity.'

\* \* \*

Campbell Muir of Innestrynich was worlds removed from both Lochbuie and Barcaldine. When still quite young he inherited a small property on the shores of Loch Awe and a great deal of ready money. With his money he bought a fleet of motor-cars, all large and powerful machines: Mercedes, Delaunay-Belleville, Napier and Panhard-Levassor. He then settled down to wage unprovoked and unrestricted guerilla warfare on his neighbours, and for that matter on anyone who incurred his easily aroused displeasure.

At first he was subject to gentle, if temporary, influences. But when he threw his bedfellow out of the house on a winter's night with a foot of snow on the ground, having first emptied her purse and hidden her shoes and stockings, it became difficult for him to find replacements. On that occasion his inhumanity was defeated by his own cook, who took the lass in by the back door as soon as he had thrown her out by the front, and 'sorted' her master properly on the following day. After that his volatile affections were transferred to the internal combustion engine for some considerable time. Many wished that they had not been so transferred. Much of Loch Awe lies in the deep cleft between steep hills, and the banks shelve down abruptly into dangerous waters. The main Glasgow–Oban road skirted the edge of the loch and was then barely wide enough for two vehicles to pass at a foot pace, let alone the forty fierce miles an hour which was Campbell Muir's slowest when he decided to visit Oban for a dram or three. He must have been the first motorised bandit to terrorise Argyll.

Those who went to his house, meaning to use sweet reason and plausible argument, were driven away by stones thrown with great force and accuracy from his library windows. Nobody ever got inside the house. He quarrelled continuously: with his own tenants, with his neighbours, with those unlucky enough to rent his water, and with the Lord Provost and Corporation of the City of Glasgow.

A farmer annoyed him. Next day the farmer's favourite milch cow was missing and could not be found. The poor beast was returned to him by rail, carriage unpaid, with a bullet hole in its head.

A retired colonel unwisely decided to try chicken farming on Campbell Muir's land. His landlord picked a quarrel with him in the bar of the Loch Awe Hotel. Ten days later, after a day spent fishing the loch, the colonel came home to find his doorstep piled high with the carcases of his fowls. Not one had been left. If there was no evidence, and none came to light, nobody had any doubt where the guilt lay. Another colonel rented some water from him. He knew all about the chicken fancier but couldn't see the red light. There was a difference of opinion over something or other. Thereafter, when the colonel went out to fish, Campbell Muir's car appeared on the opposite bank, and where the colonel cast a fly, Campbell Muir cast a stone, which was not conducive to successful angling. The colonel swore vengeance and took to carrying a hunting-crop as well as a rod, but his landlord was motorised and he was not, so the promised thrashing was never administered. But the second colonel went to law, so did the farmer, who by then had got some evidence of his cow's murder. Both cases were decided in the Sheriff-Substitute's Court and very much to the laird's disadvantage. Thereafter he was never quite free of impending litigation of one kind or another. Whatever you might think about him, Argyll was never dull when he was about.

At the Glasgow Fair Holiday it was the custom for the Lord Provost and Bailies of that fair city to cast aside their civic cares, travel to the Loch Awe Hotel, which held fishing rights on the loch, lunch festively, drink all the drams they could hold, and sally forth on the loch in the afternoon to see what they might catch. That, as a rule, was not very much, but the change and the outing was much enjoyed and much anticipated by the good burgesses of Glasgow. Till, that is to say, Campbell Muir took a hand.

He had for some time vigorously denied the right of the hotel to fish the bay opposite his house, and when people took a chance and he happened to be on the spot, he used his favourite tactic of throwing stones. He threw them far and very accurately, and had not been the least discouraged by his experience with the colonel. But on the afternoon of that Glasgow Fair Holiday, his patience, like that of a greater menace yet to come, was exhausted. A boatload of euphorious and well-drammed bailies drifted into the bay and began to fish. Campbell Muir, in the best naval tradition, fired his first shot, from a .300 express rifle, across their bows. In their happy state they didn't realise what was going on and paid no attention. His next three shots holed the boat at the waterline, passing clean through both sides. How nobody's ankle was smashed was never explained. The Lord must have taken the Corporation under His especial care. Confusion and indignation succeeded the euphoria, water welled in through six punctures and a fine flow of invective rolled across the loch, to be returned with interest and profanity by Campbell Muir. The enraged dignitaries were put ashore and returned to the hotel swearing vegeance and crying aloud for yet more drams to restore their shaken dignity. They had their compensation from the Law and most properly were awarded swingeing damages.

That same week, when driving in to Oban, Campbell Muir's Mercedes sideswiped the little Peugeot of a French girl and knocked both girl and car into the loch, at, luckily, the only shallow spot within miles. Far from going to her help, he stood up in his Mercedes, swore at her heartily, and drove on to Oban. It was a full hour before anyone came to her aid.

Even so, more human passions were again stirring in his breast. He fell in love with a really delightful girl of his own station in life, well guarded by a widowed mother and so placed that it must be matrimony or nothing. Her mother, naturally, took the very dimmest possible view of Campbell Muir as a suitor, money or no money. He was barred the house. But for the girl he wore the double glamour of the bad and the forbidden. A clandestine correspondence ensued.

One afternoon, when out in his car, he met the mother and daughter driving themselves in a little Victoria. A Victoria, by the way, was not an early make of automobile, but a small, one-horse carriage. He stopped in mid-road, climbed out and went to speak with mama. To her he apologised most profusely for any trouble he might have caused, assured her that his intentions were wholly honourable, and offered, as his suit had apparently so distressed her, to withdraw it altogether. The lady made the mistake of taking him at his face value. She descended from the Victoria to explain to him just why the match he proposed would be quite unsuitable. For one thing, she and her daughter were Roman Catholics and he . . . she got no further. Campbell Muir put an open hand under her jaw, and pushed hard. She fell into a deep bramble-filled ditch as he had intended her to. He then grabbed the not unwilling daughter, threw her into the car and was away like Young Lochinvar but much faster. And in those days the police were not motorised.

The next word that came through was to the effect that they were married in the ancient Scots manner. They had declared themselves to be man and wife before two attendants and the only garage proprietor then to be found in Oban.

Shortly after this final exploit, Campbell Muir left us. No more was heard for months and months. Eventually his wife returned to the home from which she had been reft. The last thing I heard was that he had been driving a car for a Chicago citizen called Al Capone. On the whole it did not sound improbable.

But we missed him.

# Culture

I COULDN'T for the life of me say whether we were 'cultured' or uncultured. One never heard the word much anywhere until it became '*kultur*', which carried a sinister connotation in those days. One thing is certain; whatever our culture was, we were responsible for it. There was nothing canned. We even made our own music.

Mother was better than good at the piano. Piano in those days, like sketching in watercolours and petit point, gros point too, was a recognised accomplishment for a young lady. Invitations to dine out nearly always carried the postscript '*do* bring your music'. Some, who should have known better, in whose case the P.S. was never added to the invitation, would bring theirs anyway. For which reason it was highly advisable to have the maid take the gentlemen's overcoats in the hall. Then you couldn't see and didn't know of the rolled music-sheets in the inside breastpockets which cleared you of any obligation to ask for a rendering of 'Goodbye' or 'Asleep in the Deep' or 'Tom Bowling'. These 'renderings' so pained mother, who had an exquisite musicianly ear, that she became first a whist player and later, a bridge fiend. At the piano she was wonderful. She never needed to bring her music. She carried all Chopin in her ash-blonde head. But at the bridge-table she was deplorable, and never knew it. To the very end of her days she lived under the illusion that she was a first-class bridge player. She was very bad indeed. So acute did the situation become that, when contract came in, father and I made a pact. We would NOT learn to play contract. We stuck to it.

We never did, and therefore never became involved in mother's bridge-parties.

There was always someone singing about the house. Maggie sang the traditional Hebridean songs, delightfully, in her native Gaelic. Mrs O'Callaghan favoured Gilbert and Sullivan and nearly always preferred the male solos to the female ones. 'Tit Willow' and 'I have a song to sing O!' were certain indications of good temper in the kitchen. She varied these with Irish comic ballads of the Talbot O'Farrell type (never guessing that he began life on the River Tyne and failed as a Scottish comedian before he adopted Ould Oireland and his stage name). Grandmother leaned towards Brahms and certain Jacobite songs. But our star instrumentalist, mother, refused to sing. Her own voice infuriated her. Within a radius of two miles could be found one good violinist, one poor one, an indifferent 'cellist, a brilliant flautist and an oboeist of distinction, to say nothing of half a dozen players of the piano, none of whom reached mother's standards. And we had our native bagpipes. They are an acquired taste but there is much to be said for them, especially at a distance and, very specially, played across water on a still evening.

We had, of course, every winter, a positive plethora of concerts. Whenever anyone wanted to raise money for some good cause or other, their minds always turned towards concerts. All the big kirks had their church hall, and scarcely a week went by without a grand concert of some kind or other. At each and all the programme was very much the same; a soprano, a contralto and a baritone – each sang two songs, and each had an encore in reserve which was invariably demanded. Tenors devoted themselves to Gaelic items. There would be a piper and one who recited, certainly two piano solos from the accompanist of the evening, and a chairman, usually a clerical chairman, to explain the worthiness of the cause we were assembled to support and extol the merits of each performer who, alas, seldom lived up to the encomium. Those best worth attendance were always the Gaelic concerts. There one could still hear the traditional

Hebridean music, mouth music, waulkin' songs and the like before they had been collected and frozen by the Kennedy Frasers. The choral singing was of a high standard with both a freshness and pathos entirely of its own.

As for literature, although we had no local lending library, we were not badly off. The famous Glasgow firm of printers, Maclehose, ran an excellent library service. Their books, covered with a stiff red material – there were no dust jackets in those days – with cream labels on the spine with hand-inscribed titles, could be found in every house of note in the West Highlands. Twelve new books came each fortnight in a wooden box. We also had the benefit of the most remarkable issue of cheap books in the whole history of publishing, the Nelson sevenpennies. Seven pennies bought you a novel, well printed in clear type on thin paper of good quality, bound in stiff boards and red cloth with gilt titles on the spine. The format was small and the book slipped easily into a normal pocket. They even threw in a frontispiece for the money. Mrs Humphrey Ward, A. E. W. Mason, Anthony Hope, E. W. Hornung and writers of like quality were glad to appear in the series. We took all the more pride in our sevenpennies because the two surviving partners of the firm lived among us. Thomas Nelson owned Achnacloich and his brother Ian had Glenetive. The sevenpenny made it possible to acquire, quite painlessly, some fifty readable novels every year. The last Nelson sevenpenny I saw was in a box outside a Charing Cross Road bookseller's early this year. It was priced at two shillings. It couldn't have been printed less than thirty years ago.

We did have a Literary and Scientific Society and the very thought of it brings a blush to my leathery cheek. For once, at the age of sixteen or so, I had the almighty gall to give them a talk on 'Heraldry', a subject on which I had the merest smattering of information, it could not possibly have been called knowledge, and that largely acquired from the novels of Conan Doyle rather than any recognised text-book.

Theatre had we none. Or nothing to speak of. Once in a way a touring company played a three-night stand of lurid melodrama. Two stick in the memory. *The Beautiful White Devil*, because a brutal cossack armed with a knout, made from leather bootlaces, kicked the heroine's baby so hard that the head flew off right to the back of the hall, to appreciative cries of 'Goal!' from a delirious audience. *Gipsy Jack*, because when Jack, the missing heir to the earldom, was beating the bejesus out of the villain with his bare fists, I could see the 'parson', who was to marry Jack to the heroine in the next scene, also beating the bejesus out of a flat with a rolled-up newspaper. This was intended to synchronise with each mighty uppercut landed on the villain, but as the parson was not wholly sober, the synchronisation was faulty.

Entertainers at the piano, George Grossmith senior and Corney Grain, sometimes filled the Argyllshire Gathering Hall for a single night, and on such occasions the County came from far and near. Our Oban population at the time was about six thousand.

And we, naturally, had our amateurs. They were preferable to the present-day amateur in so far as they never pretended to be other than they were, or aspired to compete with the real thing. There was no damn' nonsense about them. The shows were put on for the benefit and amusement of the cast, not the audience. In, I think, *Pip*, Ian Hay's first novel, there is a delightful account of just such a production, as well there might be. He and his family had a house on the south side of the bay called Alt-na-Craig, and all the Beiths were up to their ears in every dramatic activity. Jock, as he was then, was a remarkably good amateur actor.

But father and mother both loved the theatre and saw that we did not suffer stage starvation. Whenever there was a really outstanding play or player to be seen in the Glasgow or Edinburgh theatres, we all went down for the week-end. Thanks to that family custom, before I was sixteen I had seen Sir Henry Irving and Ellen Terry, H. B. Irving and Dorothea Baird, Fred Terry and Julia Nielson, Matheson Lang, John Martin Harvey, Marie Tempest, the Benson Company and, thrill of thrills, Lily

Elsie and Joe Coyne with George Graves in *The Merry Widow*. We did not see these fabled creatures in a magic box, we saw them in the flesh and heard their voices issuing from their own throats, not from some amplifier, and learned the true secret of Theatre, the living presence for which there is no compensation in any kind of image or simulacrum. These trips were Treats, capital T, to be discussed and dissected for weeks afterwards and valued for evermore.

When I was very young, too young in fact, I was given a toy theatre which I didn't understand or take any interest in. It was put away in a cupboard and forgotten. But after a visit to *The Breed of the Treshams* in Edinburgh, it was remembered and dug out again. It was of German origin with a suitably rococo proscenium, a red velvet curtain on rollers and a set of floats consisting of a little tin tank for kerosene and six footlights with wicks which flared and stank when lit. Four sets came with it: 'A Baronial Interior', 'Somewhere in the Forest', 'A Cottage Interior' and 'The Garden', each consisting of a backdrop and three flats a side. Before very long, after its resuscitation, it had electric floats, two battens and a dozen spots. Any kind of lighting in any colour could be laid on. The old sets were scrapped. I designed and made my own, wrote plays and performed them in as many as six different voices. At least that was the intention. I had a perfectly appreciative and permanent audience in grandmother. Her sitting-room had been originally a bedroom with a small dressing-room leading off it. The theatre stood on a table in the dressing-room doorway, which was draped with an old portière having a piece cut out of the middle in which the proscenium was placed. We did everything from pantomime to my special version of *Lear*. Both grandmother and I disapproved of the ending, so we worked out another, robbing other Shakespeare plays for suitable lines, in which Cordelia came back and took her daddy home to a comfortable fireside for the rest of his days. I was hopelessly stage-struck. I still am.

# Culture

When Mr Rankine, the barber, who was also a bailie on the town council, got some friends together and they built a picture-house, there was great excitement not only in Oban but all through Argyll. Some of us had experienced the Bioscope in London and marvelled at the train of kings and princes following Queen Victoria's coffin through the silent streets. But we were the exceptions. We read about 'the moving pictures' which sometimes got a line or two in the *Glasgow Herald*, but for the most part we were virgin soil. Nobody could have guessed that Mr Rankine, of a rather doleful cast of countenance, would release such floods of mirth and joy in a people not given to public exhibition of their emotions. But that is just what he did. May he rest in paradise for it. For he brought us the Keystone Cops. For that alone he should have had a decoration. He brought us Charlie Chase and a greater Charlie. And Hoot Gibson and Theda Bara, somewhat disapproved of, and Marie Dressler and Gloria Swanson. Above all the Keystone Cops. They were not culture, they were glory. I have sometimes wondered whether true enjoyment, in the sense of complete surrender to a play or film, might not be a special prerogative of youth. But recently our local house played a rehash of some old Hollywood comedies. The Cops, Buster Keaton, Harold Lloyd, Laurel and Hardy with, of course, the early, unpretentious Chaplin. They were just as funny as they ever were, and, what was particularly interesting, the teddy-boys and their girl-friends reacted in the same old way. None of them could have been exposed to this type of film before, but they rolled in their seats and howled with joy, just as we did fifty years ago. And on coming out one recaptured the old sensation of having laughed oneself tired. And for me, between then and the Oban days, lay, among other experiences, seven years of very hard labour as a film critic.

But to revert. That picture-house overnight jumped into the foreground of our lives. Small boys began to run around shouting, 'Bang, bang, you're deid! Bite you the dust!' There was a run on percussion caps, tin pistols and, very strangely, a decrease in illegitimate births. This was explained seriously by a doctor. When parents knew what time the film programme ended, they also knew what time their lasses ought to get home. Time once spent in the whin-bushes was spent in the Picture House where necking could only go so far and no further. Pictures became an integral part of life.

Take the case of a certain provost. He was a worthy citizen of credit and some house property. Even lawyers took off their hats to him in the street. Whenever the famous Scottish tenor Mr Neil Maclean honoured us with a recital in the Gathering Hall, the provost was sure to be on the platform and to give his civic benediction to native Gaelic song in a few well-chosen phrases, fifteen minutes of them. But the pictures . . . he was not convinced that pictures were not a little frivolous for a man in his position. He, very properly, took himself and his position seriously. The first time it happened was in Argyll Square. A wee laddie ran up to him and shouted, 'Hey, Ben!' Ben? Some mistake. Ben. . . . But it caught on. Wherever he passed there were giggles and 'Hey, Ben! Auld Ben Provost!' All the brats in the place were calling him Ben. He asked his clerk about it. A male clerk naturally. To his surprise the man swallowed, giggled, blushed, hummed and hawed and rushed out of the room. The provost wondered if the whole world wasn't going daft. But when the provost did finally surrender to the Picture House, as Bailie Rankine's guest, he saw the cross-eyed Ben Turpin and all was made clear to him.

People soon became addicts. Colonel Jimmy was among the first. He became a connoisseur of westerns. Horses and horseman-ship were his meat, and part of his weekly time with grandmother was occupied by a description of the last film he had seen. People talked about their films then as the present-day TV lunatic talks TV to the exclusion of everything else. Jimmy's conversation had a most unlooked-for result. One evening when father had just come in, grandmother fixed him with her eagle eye and said, 'John, I wish to go to the Picture House.'

Sensation! Grandmother had fared no further than the garden for two or three years and then only in high summer. It was now midwinter. Father was so taken aback that he asked, 'But . . . Mother, how will you get there?'

'That,' said grandmother, being very grand indeed, 'will be for you to arrange.' And, as far as she was concerned, the matter was closed. For the rest of us, it had only begun.

Grandmother was then eighty-one, frail, a cripple to arthritis and subject to severe colds. A matinée was decided upon for obvious reasons. Jimmy was detailed as gentleman in waiting. My part, which earned me a free seat, was to run her wheel-chair down to the cinema and have it ready when she got there. Father consulted with the manager and arranged just where the chair would go in the auditorium. Maggie had to attend at the door of the cinema and lift grandmother from the carriage to the chair. She trusted Maggie more than anyone else for that duty. Before the day her fur coat, black sealskin with a sable collar, was shaken to get rid of the moth-balls and aired to get rid of their smell. She had not used it for years. And when the day came there was such a wrapping up in shawls, filling of hot-water bottles, putting of restorative smelling-salts into black velvet bags and consultation about bonnets (even Mrs O'Callaghan was brought in on that), as had never been known before. There was also a secret, hidden flask with a dram inside just in case of real emergency. And when it happened, it all went off with the smooth precision of a royal progress. The film, to Jimmy's disgust, was a silent version of *The Merry Widow* starring Miss Mae Murray, then publicised as 'The girl with the bee-stung lips'. Attended by the manager and the whole family, grandmother was wheeled to the agreed place (I'm not sure they didn't hold the film for her), and graciously permitted the programme to begin. Tea was specially organised for her, an amenity never before offered to patrons of the Picture House. Miss McGeachy, who played the harmonium on Sundays in the Tabernacle of an obscure but Protestant sect, and hammered out 'atmospheric' music on an aged upright in the Picture House for the rest of the week, played as she had seldom played before or since. Her brio was tremendous.

I sometimes think that the very name of the Picture House was significant. It was *not* a Granada, a Florida, a Regal, a Picturedrome, an Electric Palace or a Pantheon. It was just a Picture House. It was plain, simple and adequate to our simple needs.

'The Merry Widow' was followed by a custard-pie comedy of some sort and a travel feature. We did not run to a newsreel in those days. Then grandmother was wheeled out to hold a kind of levée in the foyer. News of her expedition had spread far and wide and people had just 'dropped in when passing' to congratulate her on her enterprise, which congratulations she received much as the Dear Queen must have received a deputation from her loyal Commons. She was then taken outside where a further surprise, engineered by father, was waiting for her. Mr MacDougall, the ironmonger, who also kept a garage, had recently bought a second-hand Daimler limousine for hiring purposes, and there it stood outside the door, its interior lit up, flowers in its silver vase and Mr MacDougall himself with a visored cap in his hand, waiting to open the door for grandmother. It was her first journey in a motor vehicle of any kind.

She took both experiences in her stride, so to speak, but the car made by far the deeper impression. Next spring she used it several times, firmly rejecting any substitute. It was the Daimler or nothing. And no driver other than Mr MacDougall himself would be considered for an instant. It said much for his kindness of heart that, although he was a comparatively wealthy man with an ever-increasing business, he never failed to respond to grandmother's summons, or to accept the half-crown she graciously tendered to him at the journey's end.

The film, she said somewhat cryptically, was enjoyable but not *real*. She had only wanted to know what exactly it was that plainly gave Colonel Jimmy and me so much pleasure and amusement. Now she could understand better what we were talking about. But once was enough. She never repeated the experience.

As for the plastic arts, we had Miss Janet and only Miss Janet. But they were more extensively practised than any other, if with less success. Every year innumerable water-colours were perpetrated by innumerable ladies till they became, socially, a source of some embarrassment. Nobody really wanted them but they were for ever being sold (at five shillings a time) at church bazaars and sales of work. These, especially in the Episcopal Church which had plunged into debt, were legion. If the drawings failed to sell, they were raffled off. Sixpenny tickets. So nobody could very well avoid owning a 'Sunset over Mull', a 'Dunollie Castle and Thunderclouds' or 'The Bay from Pulpit Hill'. They just weren't worth framing. But each and every artist had her share of the vanity of all artists and kept an eye on the distribution. They knew who had bought, or won, the masterpiece, and expected to see it displayed when they came to tea. Mother solved the problem in her own canny way. She bought, she never took raffle tickets, and her purchases were governed by the size of the painting. They had to fit her frame. There was one frame hung in the drawing-room, in which the picture was constantly changed. When Mrs A. came to call she was delighted to see her 'Rain over Kerrera' in a place of honour. Next week Miss B. would be no less pleased to see her 'Three Kittens and a Hen' lending life to an otherwise undistinguished collection. When any two artists were present simultaneously, the work of a third was on view, and whatever disappointment they felt at not seeing their own work was mitigated by the pleasure they derived from castigating the work of another. This sharp practice on mother's part continued for years, and she never once slipped up.

But of true creative artists, Miss Janet apart, we had none. The novels and plays of Ian Hay, the novels of his sister Janet Beith, were both still in the future. Andrew Lang and the no less celebrated Professor Blackie dwelled among us from time to time, and Miss Marie Corelli honoured us once for a whole fortnight, exhibiting, as we thought, a most indecent curiosity as to what there might be underneath a kilt.

In sum, perhaps not very much, but for a remote little community, rather outside the world as it wagged, not altogether despicable. At least it was active and individual. The wholesale standardisation of first radio and later TV, was mercifully absent. We talked about what interested us, what we had experienced, and not what some haphazard collection of publicists had said last night in a panel game.

# Fun and Games

OUR Highland Games had the simplest of origins. Some Maclaine of Lochbuie would wager a few gold pieces that his man Ian Beg could put a stone farther than MacDougall of MacDougall's Donald Dubh. A meeting place would be arranged for the contest and when it was over the young folk would run races, jump, and toss the caber, clan against clan, in friendly rivalry. And when the sun went down there would be the dancing and the singing that was to be expected when the young people came together; the bard, or *sennachie*, would deliver himself of a poem in praise of the victor, and food and drink would be forthcoming at the Chief's expense. It was no more than that.

From such simple beginnings, the Highland Games of today have developed into second-class athletic fixtures for professionals competing for money prizes. Some of them make a regular autumn occupation of it. They do have some local renown, especially the giants who toss the caber, but not very much. They are, as a rule, not local men. But, for all that, things still happen at Highland Games which don't happen anywhere else and give a strong, local, Highland flavour to what can be a very pleasant day's amusement: the piping competitions which never cease from dawn to dusk; the Highland dancing, which alone is worth going to see, and the tossing of the caber. Also, perhaps, if you are lucky, you may see one Highland regiment pitted against another in the tug-of-war, and that is war indeed, or against those very solid men of muckle might, the Glasgow City Police, who are Highlanders to a man. There are many worse ways of spending your time.

All the big meetings – they are gatherings, meetings or games according to local usage – have a strong social side to them. When travel was difficult, and roads even more so, kinsfolk who lived at opposite ends of the county could be certain of meeting at least once a year at the gathering and watching their offspring partner one another at the ball. Many a girl first met boy at a gathering ball. And if Lochbuie no longer had an Ian Beg to put his money on, he had the pleasure of seeing and meeting his own kind from all over the county.

The Argyllshire Gathering of my boyhood was, naturally, very much a Campbell affair. Each annual gathering was presided over by a Chieftain elected by the Gathering Committee, and as often as not that Chieftain was the Duke of Argyll.

On the morning of the games, which were held towards the end of September, the chiefs and lairds would assemble soon after breakfast in Argyll Square. They would then be marshalled, and the Duke, preceded by a blast of fifty or sixty pipers playing 'The Campbells are Coming', and followed by his vassals and tacksmen, would march off to the games ground. There would be Campbells of Argyll, Airds and Ardchattan; Campbells of Breadalbane, Barcaldine and Ballieviolan; Campbells of Dunstaffnage, Inverawe and Lochnell; Campbells of Succoth, Saddell and Glassary; Campbells of Kilberry, Arduine and . . . memory fails. Anyhow Campbells galore. Many of them had their sons and heirs at their sides; all were tweedily jacketed, all were Campbelly kilted and plaided, each with brogues on his feet, a *cromach*★ in his hand and having a sprig of bog-myrtle, the Campbell badge, in his bonnet.

Even so, the green tartans did not have it all their own way.

In the same procession you might see MacDougall of MacDougall and Maclean of Duart, chiefs in their own right, with Ardgour and Lochbuie. There would be Stewarts of Achnacone and Coll, Stuart of Achara, MacAlpine Downie of

★ A long hazel stick with a crook like a crozier.

Appin, MacDonalds from both Dunach and Taynuilt, Camerons from Ardsheil and Inverailort, Malcolm of Poltalloch and visiting lairds from the east and the north, and no man marched behind the Duke who was not by birth or inheritance a Highland laird.

Having stressed the social character of this function, you may wonder just what part the womenfolk of this resplendent array might have to act. Small parts for the most of them. They either waited for the arrival of the procession at the games ground or came later. In Highland Balls and Highland Games the emphasis lies on the masculine gender. They are no place for feminists. By day the male wears kilt and plaid with such panache as he can muster. The lady is content with tweeds or, perhaps, a tartan skirt. At night, he peacocks it in the full glory of tartan, velvet and lace, of gold buckles and jewelled dirks and diamond brooches; she wears a simple white ball-dress with a sash of her tartan, like the ribbon of an Order, over her left shoulder. That is customary rather than *de rigueur* and most becoming to a young girl. And when you have added in the mess uniforms of one or two Highland regiments and the dark blue and gold of the Navy, why, you have a very gorgeous ballroom indeed compared with the white tie and tails of the Sassenach dancers.

At the games ground very few in the stands paid any attention to what was going on in the arena. That was for the benefit of the general public, who sat in the open round the ring or stood on a rocky eminence which dominated the western end of the ground and made an excellent natural grandstand. In the enclosure, Campbells shook hands with Campbells, non-Campbells with non-Campbells, at first. Later, after a visit to the refreshment rooms below the stand, Campbells shook hands with non-Campbells and *vice versa*. This queer type of tension must sound unbelievable to the outsider, but it was there. It most certainly was there.

At one gathering, two non-Campbell boys (I was one of them) were walking round with a Campbell girl, and none of us had reached our eighth birthday. The Duke of Argyll, he who married the old Queen's daughter, came up to us and stopped. He was a very fine-looking old man with a great shock of white hair and the profile of a Roman emperor. He looked the part of Mac Calein Mor and, at a guess, enjoyed it.

'Hah,' said the Duke. 'Now this is splendid! Campbells and Stewarts all getting on like a house on fire! Now I'll tell you what we'll do. Duncan [Duncan was a Stewart], you take the oak-leaves out of your bonnet [oak-leaves were the Stewart badge] and give them to Mary. And Mary will give you her bog-myrtle, and you'll wear each other's badges for the rest of the day.'

'Why?' asked Mary.

'As a sign of friendship,' said the Duke, 'and to please me. You are friends, aren't you?'

'Y-y-yes, sir,' said Duncan, a thought doubtfully, and took off his bonnet. Small boys didn't disobey a Duke of Argyll then, even if they were called Stewart. He took out the oak-leaves and handed them to Mary. She, being of the deadlier sex, had no hesitations or compunctions about disobeying her Chief. She spat on the leaves, dropped them on the ground, stamped her heel on them, made a face at the Duke and ran off. Such was the operation of atavism *circa* 1904. Yet Duncan and Mary were friends, very good friends. We three were of like age, went to the same parties and never had rows among ourselves. That incident couldn't have taken place outside Argyllshire.

The other great meetings – Inverness's Northern Meeting, for instance, which was probably more important and certainly more fashionable – were never quite so dominated by one clan. Because the best grouse shooting was to be had east of Argyllshire, the eastern moors naturally attracted the wealthier and more distinguished tenants and sportsmen. Inverness was the capital of the Highlands from time immemorial. It was also the depot of the Cameron Highlanders, which regiment was then regarded more as Cameron of Lochiel's private army than as something belonging to the Crown. But that was not Lochiel's privilege. The only subject permitted a private army was the Duke of Atholl, a privilege he still holds. Inverness drew all the Grants from Strathspey, the Mackintoshes from Moy, the Sutherlands from Dunrobin, the Frasers from Beauly, the MacLeod, Mackinnon and Macdonald chieftains from Skye, and there were usually young members of the Royal Family at the northern meetings. The programme was the same, the underlying idea was much the same, the idea of the grand annual get-together of Inverness county and places north, but Inverness was distinctly grander, whatever the Campbells might like to think.

Of all the gatherings, to my own way of thinking, the most pleasing is that at Aboyne in Deeside. Aboyne is a Gordon affair presided over by the Marquess of Huntly. It has a strongly local flavour, and Huntly, advised, and very well advised, by Sir Thomas Innes of Learney, the Lord Lyon King of Arms, Scotland's chief Herald, has reintroduced some picturesque customs which were allowed to lapse elsewhere. At Aboyne, each laird is preceded onto the field by his personal banner displaying his coat of arms, adding colour and dignity to the games as a whole. The banners are grouped round Huntly's own standard, three gold boars' heads on a blue ground for Gordon. He made a marked improvement in another direction. During Victorian days it became the custom for girl dancers to wear a kilt and sporran, with tartan stockings and velvet coats of the same cut as the men. One can only suppose the Victorians thought they looked 'cute'. But they looked horrible. Female legs in kilt and stockings look all wrong. The stockings and the edge of the kilt break the line of the leg twice. Lord Huntly went back to earlier days and decreed a loose skirt topped by a bolero-type of jacket over a blouse. The result is charming, and has restored a truly feminine grace and elegance to the Highland dancing which had been missing far too long. Other games are following his excellent example.

Then comes Braemar. Braemar is the most publicised of all the gatherings. It attracts more foreign and overseas visitors than all the others put together, because it has become to all intents and purposes the personal affair of the Royal Family. Farquharsons of Invercauld come there, and Lord Aberdeen. Also the Duke of Fife, but he is a member of the Family. Lesser lairds are few and far between.

I must confess to disliking this gathering very much indeed.

There is a bad spirit abroad in the land which, for want of a better term, may be called regiolatry. It has nothing to do with respect for the monarchy or loyalty to the throne. It is sired by curiosity out of familiarity, the wrong kind of familiarity, nurtured by that section of the Press who regard royalty not so much as their business as their prey. While it pretends to popularise Royal personages and insolently calls them by their Christian names, it only succeeds in debasing both the individual and the office. They want to demonstrate that Royal persons are just the same as Mrs Snooks at No. 3. They are not. And if they were, the whole of their tradition, training and upbringing would be a complete nonsense. But it uplifts the hearts of morons to think that their Mavis is no different from a princess because she likes the same pop songs. It is rather the attitude of the fan club to the star but infinitely more impertinent.

Regiolatry has made it necessary to put screens up in places round Balmoral Castle to foil the binoculars of those who lie on the hillside and spy on their Queen's privacy. Regiolatry crams its practitioners into the Crathie Church to 'get a good view' of the Royal Family and fills the churchyard with sightseers when the party comes out. But at the Braemar Games there are no obstructions. People sit with binoculars glued on the Royal box for hours on end. You can watch them, like leopards in a cage, for an entire afternoon if such is your disposition.

Regiolatry allows unsatisfactory servants to make large sums of money by publishing their experiences in Royal households. Worse still, it has compelled the Queen Mother, that most gracious and charming lady who has served her country as few have served it, to take legal action to prevent a disloyal servant from publishing his 'memoirs' of her daughter. Such a situation could not arise unless those who ought to know better were prepared to pay large sums for 'Royal revelations'. At Braemar, as at Crathie, regiolatry is open and rampant. One hopes that the foreign element outnumbers the native, for certainly it is a thing clean against the Highlander's nature and abominable in his eyes.

But, just in case someone wants to go to Braemar and prove me wrong, and I hope he may, a word of warning. Elsewhere, when Royalty enters a public place, it is the custom to stand up. This does not, repeat does *not*, apply to Braemar. Some few years ago, just when the Royal car was passing our seats by the ringside, I followed the normal custom and rose. Instantly there was a furious bellow from behind. 'Sit doon, ye auld b——!' The auld b—— sat doon so fast that he nearly missed the bench altogether. But there is reason in the local ruling. The ringside ground is flat, not terraced, and one stander-up blocks the view of many.

The true heroes of our Highland Games are not the beefy caber-tossers and wrestlers. There are usually three of them. They sit together in a huddle round a small wooden table inside the ring. They have notebooks and pencils. When it is wet, and it can be very wet, they huddle inside their plaids, rain-darkened, like three tortoises in their shells. And there they sit, listening, listening, listening. They are the judges of pipe music. And whatever the weather the pipers pipe ceaselessly, one pibroch succeeding another, to the very end of the meeting. It must be a difficult and wearing task whose rewards are beyond the comprehension of lesser men.

You have probably gathered by now that I am a convinced old Tory Royalist. Not a square but a cube. But when you look back over fifty years and see what dictators, presidents and politicians have done to this wretched world, the advantage of a trained head of state, a supra-political referee, seems enormous. Nor can I see that any country except perhaps the USSR has gained in prestige or material prosperity by abolishing its hereditary rulers. Here, we of the Highlands and that very long memory, look at things slightly differently from our English partners in Britain. The English have not and never have had any sense of dynastic loyalty. The last real

Englishman to rule England was Harold, who died like the hero he was at Senlac about nine hundred years ago. Since then the English have accepted Normans, Angevins, Plantagenets, Welsh Tudors, Scots Stuarts, Dutch Williams and German Geordies. They don't seem to care. The last Plantagenets, Edward IV and Richard III, were almost English, but not a hundred per cent.

We Highlanders, at least most of us, have never felt like that. We had our Stuarts and stuck by them and died for them in a brutal massacre at Drummossie perpetrated by the fat scion of a frightened dynasty, Cumberland. (And what was done in the Highlands after Culloden by government troops, Lowland Scots among them, doesn't bear thinking about.) 1746 isn't a long way back by our kind of reckoning.

# Scandalum Magnatum

THE foregoing chapters ought to have prepared the way for this. Both the Games and the Picture House were intimately involved, and it was the very biggest typhoon in a teacup to blow up in Argyll during the times I lived there. Today, nobody would bother about it. We had the Campbell Muir excitements, an elopement or two, and there had been certain illicit loves. There had been my own little trouble at a dance when I saw, as I thought, a certain undesirable 'forcing his attentions', as we then said, on a most desirable and, as I thought, reluctant maiden. I kicked his bottom from behind, got a black eye in the fracas which ensued, and the maiden married him next Christmas. It was the first intimation of the deplorable fact that chivalry does not always pay. One can't be expected to know that at sixteen. Empiricism is all.

The storm centre of our typhoon was Kenneth Maclaine, Lochbuie's son and heir. Kenneth was a year or two older than I was, which, even then, made a big difference in the world of teens and early twenties. But, thanks to his good-natured tolerance we got on very well when we met, which was not often. None the less, Kenneth always had his place in the category of my friends when I did any such mental accounting.

Lochbuie brought him up with the complete disregard of expense which he considered right and proper to a Highland Chief. Kenneth was encouraged to think that nothing would be expected from him save that he should succeed to Lochbuie and Lochbuie Castle, marry suitably, and continue a line which, if you were to believe the Lochbuie bards, stretched back to the Seventh

Day of Creation. It was said that the Lochbuies had their private ark during the flood and grounded on the top of Ben More about the same time as Noah found the peak of Ararat. Kenneth, therefore, toiled not neither did he spin. He never attempted to enter any profession and thoroughly enjoyed the happy outdoor life of sport and exercise and all the amenities provided by an admiring father and devoted family. What he did not know, and was never allowed to know, till it was far too late, was that the ancestral acres were mortgaged to the last boulder, and that there was another mortgage on the castle itself, practically no money in the bank, a diminishing income and every probability of foreclosure within the next few years. Prudence had no place in Lochbuie's nature, and in its room there was a double measure of hospitality and hedonism.

When, unknown to Lochbuie, his unhappy lawyers enlightened Kenneth on the real situation, he took stock of himself with shrewdness and sense. His assets were a very real charm, good looks and figure, a pleasing singing voice, and the quality of being immediately noticed and liked in any company he cared to keep. He also played the piano well. Obviously the only sphere in which such assets might be swiftly realised was – the Theatre.

Gigolos had not then been invented, and even if they had been, Kenneth was far too fundamentally honest to make a hit in that occupation. He had the double misfortune of being a gentleman both by birth and inclination. When he decided to take the plunge, he was not thinking so much of fame for himself as money for the ever hungry mortgagees. The steely egocentricity of the born star was not in his nature. But, as he very well knew, the profession has never conceded a millimetre to noble birth and never will. It demands ability at the lowest level and genius at the highest. A small part player in the West End of London in those days would think himself passing rich on seven pounds a week, a sum the mortgagees would sneer at. Engagements were few and reputations had to be built. It was not then enough to howl, wriggle and weep at moronic teenage audiences. The only possible short cut to money that Kenneth could see lay in music hall.

At this juncture he came to consult father. Father, who always automatically approved of anyone who was trying to get ahead under his own steam, neither suggested that he, Kenneth, was mad, nor suggested a clerkship in an insurance office or a bank. To anyone who had led the life Lochbuie provided for Kenneth, a clerkship was only another way of spelling Hell. Some years before, father had been called in to advise Harry Lauder on the purchase of a certain estate in south Argyll. He told Lauder not to touch it, but soon found out that he had been expected to confirm a decision already taken. His advice was ignored, Lauder bought and in due course regretted his purchase. But each took a strong liking for the other and thereafter father was always free of Lauder's dressing-room whenever their paths chanced to cross. Without telling Kenneth, my father wrote to Lauder about him. Lauder refused to advise without having seen Kenneth, but promised that if he worked up an act and found himself an engagement, and if it were at all possible, he, Lauder, would watch the act and advise when he had something to go upon. And in due time all these things came to pass.

Kenneth left Argyllshire and disappeared. None of us paid much attention to music hall. We had nothing of the kind nearer than Glasgow, and ladies, real ladies, would no more have thought of being seen in a music hall than they would have thought of going into a pub for a pint of mild and bitter. So the appearance of Kenneth Maclaine, Scotland's singing star, at the Tivoli, Hull, or the Empire, Wigan, escaped notice altogether; and even if anyone had noticed the similarity of names, none of us would have believed it possible for One of Us so to demean himself.

Harry Lauder was as good as his word. He saw Kenneth at South Shields, approved of what he saw (it never attempted to infringe the Lauder copyright), suggested certain changes in the act and even took the trouble to rehearse them with Kenneth. He wrote father a terse but favourable report. Scotland's singing star had it in him.

The Scots then held that there was a close alliance between the Theatre and the Devil. At least that was the Presbyterian view. The invasion of the stage by gentlefolk and the counter-attack of the stage on society had never been mounted as far as Argyllshire was concerned. Miss Lily Elsie was, it appeared, the sister-in-law of Sir George Bullough of Rhum, which gave her some slight claim for serious consideration, but, by and large, actresses were believed to be immoral, and actors, except Sir Henry Irving, although they might be asked to share a stag lunch at one's club, were ineligible for private hospitality.

Our good friend Doctor Anderson had a most respectable and efficient housekeeper, an Englishwoman called Fish. She had been looking after him for some years when he happened to discover, and to his immense delight, that Mrs Fish when young had created a rôle in the original production of 'The Mikado' at the Savoy Theatre. Pitti Sing, I think. So far from boasting about it, Mrs Fish implored him to forget all about her awful past. If it were noised abroad, she said, it would compromise her chances of other work in Scotland. Possessed of this secret, I can remember looking at Mrs Fish, who was not, by then, exactly photogenic, and thinking that it would be difficult to imagine anyone sinning with her, or even pouring champagne into her slippers.

In excuse for our backwardness, please remember that we were both remote and inaccessible.

One day a notice was posted up outside the Oban Picture House. It stated briefly that no films would be played during the Gathering week, but a company of variety artists (details later) would give performances twice nightly. Because it had never happened before, it was noticed and regretted by film fans. Probably some pierrot troupe trying to cash in on the Gathering crowds. But when the promised details were forthcoming and it was known that Kenneth Maclaine, Scotland's singing star, supported by six other names, all totally unknown to us, would appear, the uproar began.

In another age, to which he really belonged, Kenneth's problem would have been comparatively simple. He, like many another Scots gentleman before him, would have taken a commission in the Imperial Service, or in Russia, or France, and worked out his salvation in his own *métier* like the Counts Keith in Austria, who descended from the famous marshal of that name. There were Counts Douglas in Sweden, Mackensens in Germany, Macdonalds and de Lauristons in France where the Montgomeries, Lord Eglinton's family, had commanded the Scottish Archer Guard, and so forth. Kenneth was soon to fight a war, and fight it with gallantry and distinction, but he did not then know it. Meanwhile he sang sentimental and gay ditties on the public stage. To Argyllshire then, it was as it might be today were a Royal princess to sign on as a stripper at the Windmill Theatre. Down in the south, as we well knew, money was nudging at the elbow of birth, but whatever happened elsewhere, we meant to uphold our standards. We hadn't really very much else to uphold.

By 1912 the telephone had made its bow and was beginning to be generally used. From the moment of The Announcement, ours was never silent. Mother spent half her afternoons at it.

'What *can* you make of it?'

'Terrible! Who would have expected Kenneth of all people to *disgrace* his family?'

'But you aren't going to *go*, are you?'

'Shocking business altogether. Very sorry for the Lochbuies.'

'Have you booked seats? I have. Wouldn't miss this for *worlds*.'

'We aren't going. My husband says one can't support this kind of thing.'

'A Lochbuie paintin' his face and prancin' on the stage! Never heard of such a thing!'

'And the Gathering week too! D'you suppose he'll come to the balls? I'll take jolly good care our Fiona doesn't dance with him.'

And much more in the same vein.

There was practically no other subject of conversation. Father made his position clear from the outset.

'You don't mean to say you're going to this exhibition?'

'I've a dozen tickets,' said father, 'and I don't mean to waste them. Besides, how do you know he isn't good?'

'Good? How can he be good?'

'You can't tell till you see him. And if you do, you'd better book soon if you want to get in at all.'

On the eve of the Gathering I ran into the fount and origin of this glorious stramash (a Scots word for how-d'ye-do or hoo-ha) in the Station Hotel. He, at least, was unperturbed and wholly unrepentant. With him were two of the supporting artistes, a red-headed *chanteuse* of forty or so, made up to kill, and a very pretty little dancer of half that age with blue eyes and linten locks.

'Come and tell me what they're saying,' said Kenneth, and introduced me to both ladies. The lounge was full of assembled Campbells, lairds, wives, sons and daughters all set for the Games. We talked under a battery of looks. Some approving, some envious (I said that the dancer was pretty), some lustful, some wondering, but most of them plain black.

I told him.

'Stay away?' He was laughing. 'That's the one thing they won't do. You ought to see the box-office figures. We're practically sold out already. Not so bad for a first venture into management. Perhaps they'll come in disguise or creep in late hoping not to be seen, but come they will. You won't be able to keep them out. All that worries me is that they may sit on their hands. Won't break my heart if they do, but these lads and lasses with me wouldn't like it. I've warned them, but I hope it won't happen. When you do come – I take it you are coming?'

'Father has a dozen tickets for tonight.'

'Splendid. Just like him. Well, when you do come, beat your hands together as loudly as you possibly can. Now let's all have a drink.'

By then I had been promoted to the occasional dram taken in public. Kenneth had changed. His former diffidence had dropped away. He was slightly fuller in the face, which had acquired that smoothness of skin that comes from rubbing off greasepaint and cream with a rough towel, and he seemed altogether confident and assured. The Campbells continued to look. When I reached home, mother also had a look ready.

'I hear on good authority that you have been drinking whisky in public with "that swaggering young Lochbuie".' She stressed the quotes.

'It didn't take long for that to get around.'

'No . . . and I've had it from three separate sources.'

'Is that all?'

'Quite enough. I like your friend Kenneth, but the sooner this nonsense is over, the better pleased I'll be. Quite sensible people seem to have gone off their heads.'

In the event it was exactly as Kenneth had predicted. The house was barely half full when the curtain rose. His supporting company were adequate and professional, even if some of the gags were not . . . well, not *quite*. For himself, he reserved the spot before the interval, by which time it was 'standing room only' and none of that worth speaking about; then he appeared in the last number before the final curtain.

He took his first number in full Highland evening dress with all the traditional accoutrements. This was to avoid comparison with the traditional Scots comedian as exemplified by his mentor Harry Lauder. He allowed himself one dig at his audience when he explained that in England he used a 'lead in' to the act which explained to the English just what things were for. The *skian dubh* for cutting up roast venison, and the dirk for gralloching a stag or, gently fingering the edge, for cutting Campbell throats, which had once been a favourite occupation of the Maclaines. From the multitudinous Campbells in the house there came what can only be described as an incredulous snort. But after that he got down to the business of putting over three numbers, light

Scottish songs written specially for him, with all his considerable charm and attack. The third won a real round of applause from half those present, and some half-hearted clapping from the ranks of Campbell Tuscany. When the curtain fell on his third call and the house lights came up, there was nothing to do but stay seated. The Picture House then had no facilities for refreshment and the nearest pub was some considerable distance away. Mother amused herself by counting the heads who had sworn that nothing would drag them inside the place. There were also those who had 'pulled their hats about their brows' in hope of passing unrecognised, but it was very clear that curiosity had conquered social consciousness. Some of the faces were pretty red.

But once 'discovered', in the theatrical sense, they made the best of it. They had to. They had submitted to outrage and were secretly hoping for more. They didn't get what they expected. Kenneth's last number was called 'Monty from Monte Carlo', which he positively slammed across in a top hat, a plum-coloured evening-dress suit with yellow bow-tie and waist-coat and a gold-headed Malacca cane. It was the type of song that reached its apogee in 'Gilbert the Filbert', which Basil Hallam used to sing at the Palace before he was killed in action. But by this time Scotland's singing star had the audience where he wanted it. They were responding to a very competent artist and had forgotten the laird's son with the painted face, prancin' on the stage though he most undoubtedly was. The last curtain came down to real, wholehearted applause. And the first house departed to prepare for the Gathering Ball with something to talk about.

Hostility, if it had been anything more than a token hostility at any time, disappeared. Kenneth had won. Not only that, he had six hundred pounds clear profit, all salaries and expenses paid, to prove it. Even to mortgagees that was an appreciable sum. And that venture into management and the lion's den needed courage.

A few years later I was plodding through a filthy trench in the Ypres Salient on the way to a twenty-four-hour tour of duty in the battery observation post. Behind were an orderly and two signallers with rations and gear for the night. At a trench junction just ahead, a figure clambered out of a deep dugout in the side of the trench. It wore a goatskin jerkin, a tin hat and respirator and looked just as anonymous, standardised by the universal mud and squalor which masked everyone in that depressing neighbourhood, as any other, except for one thing. It carried a cromach, something one didn't expect to see in a Flanders trench. It stopped and leaned on the cromach in a certain way you will see at every Highland Games. And it was Kenneth. By that time he had acquired a majority, a wound stripe and the French Croix de Guerre with Palm.

'Good God!' he shouted. 'Well . . . I told you they'd come in, didn't I?' and fell to laughing like a drain. There was no time for more than a passing hail and, although we did arrange to meet, the meeting fell through for one or other of wartime's innumerable emergencies.

One heard later that he had married a kinswoman of Lady Constance Stewart Richardson, a lady whose dancing, in the genre of Miss Maud Allen, had created as big a sensation in London as Kenneth's adventure in Argyll. Later we heard that he had been awarded the Military Cross and Bar; but, whatever his service record, the bravest thing he ever did was to face a County, assembled for the express purpose of damning him, in Mr Rankine's Picture House.

He died, shortly after the war, from the effects of his wounds: a gallant Highland gentleman.

# Of Things That Go
# Bump in the Night

It is said by those who should know that it would be wrong to write about the West Highlands and say nothing about our ghosts and legends.

It has been always something of a disappointment that, despite every readiness to see and to believe, nothing has ever happened to me personally which might induce a belief in ghosts. Not a moan, not a howl, never a rattling of chains or a White Lady gliding across a Moonlit Lawn. Nothing.

This is all the more frustrating because one of my forefathers was a notorious warlock and the proof of his wizardry may be found in Aubrey's *Brief Lives*. He was a cavalry colonel and would seem to have been a pretty good one. He commanded the body-guard of King Charles II on the field of Worcester, and got his master safe away from the battle despite the Cromwellian cavalry. He shared the King's exile and restoration. Eventually he returned to Scotland. There, perhaps from sheer boredom, and Duffus must have been pretty deadly after the glamour and gaieties of Whitehall, he took up what would now be described as occult studies but then had the more picturesque name of 'Nigromancy'. Retired cavalry colonels are apt to be idiosyncratic. Aubrey, like all founder members of the Royal Society, had his correspondents all over the country. His friend in Edinburgh, a doctor, wrote to him that at a rout, my forebear was heard to exclaim, 'Horses and Hattocks!' whereafter he turned about three times and was no more seen.

He was next heard of 'in the cellars of the French King, drinking wine from a silver cup'. Whether the 'French King' implied Versailles, where he was no stranger, or whether it was the name of some Edinburgh howff or drinking den, is not known. At any rate his gifts were not transmitted to any of his descendants, with the possible exception of Mrs Elinor Glyn of 'Three Weeks' fame who was certainly gifted with eternal youth. It is more likely that this descendant is just too much of the earth, earthy, to be susceptible to spiritual phenomena.

All the same, inexplicable things have happened to those I have known personally, people whose integrity was not for a moment in doubt. Here are two examples of what I mean.

In 1912 four friends came to camp with me at Duror, a small village on the shores of Loch Linnhe. It was a glorious late summer that year and we revelled in heat and sunshine all the time we were there. We shared a bell-tent pitched beside a deep pool of the Duror River, which would be better described as a big burn than a real river. The pool was deep enough for bathing. To the north and east we were sheltered by a scrubby little wood of hazel and alder. A kindly farmer's wife – the farm was five hundred yards away – supplied us with butter, eggs, bread of her own baking and soda scones and oatcakes. The general merchant in Duror, who sold everything from home-cured bacon to brass rowlocks, from March Brown trout-flies to liquorice sticks, afforded all our other necessities. Somebody would get up early and catch enough small brown trout for breakfast; somebody else cooked them and a third washed up. Those simple chores apart, we were free as air. Loch Linnhe, a good deal warmer than the river, provided salt-water bathing.

On the far side of the water, opposite our tent door, was a round mound that might have been a Pictish broch. We were all as happy as kings or sixteen-year-old schoolboys, whichever you please.

After ten days it had been arranged that I should take a cricket team of eleven public-school boys to play the newly formed sports club at Kinlochleven. The British Aluminium Company's Kinlochleven works were almost brand new. A small village had been built for employees and executives in that very remote spot and some kind of communal life and entertainment was being organised by Mr Edward Morrison, the factor. It was a two days' match with a concert and dance in the middle. Only two of the camping party came with me. The others, non-cricketers, stayed in camp and we agreed to come straight back after the cricket for a final night together before striking camp for good and all.

After the match we went back to Duror only to find the camp deserted. There was a note pinned to the tent pole which said that they had both to leave sooner than expected and would write about it. It was unlike either of them to bolt in that kind of way. However, we three spent the night as usual, struck camp the next morning, tidied up, travelled to Connell Ferry together and there split up. The customary bread-and-butter letters arrived for father and mother, but no mention was made of the defection. I saw Charles Winchester at the beginning of the winter term at school. The other, Gerry Hedderwick, had been at prep school with me, but afterwards went to Loretto. Charles, the son of an Edinburgh lawyer, had always intended to be a soldier. He was commissioned in the Royal Scots a year or two later and died, very gallantly, at Loos. Charles was a very sane, level-headed young Scot and the last kind of person to panic. When I asked him what had happened and he answered, rather sheepishly, 'Sheer funk,' it didn't make sense.

'Funk? But what of?'

'Nothing at all,' said Charles. 'That was the awful part of it.'

That Christmas I spent a few days with Jerry Hedderwick's family in Glasgow. Jerry, by far the more articulate of the two, described what actually did happen. They had turned in at about eleven o'clock that night. It had been a hot, sunny day and was followed by a warm, moonlit night. As usual the tent flaps had been left wide open, so that they could lie on their palliasses inside and look over the pool to the hills beyond. After half an hour Charles complained of feeling cold and took an extra blanket from one of the unoccupied palliasses. It did no good and Jerry, who had been half dozing, suddenly was wide awake and cold, and with the cold came fear.

'I knew that there was nothing to be afraid of, what could there be in a place like that? There wasn't a sound except the rustle of water from the pool and the call of a cock grouse higher up the hill. But I was scared, almost sweating with fear and somehow I knew, without exchange of a word, that Charles was just as scared as I was. Neither of us could sleep, neither of us could get warm. I thought about getting up and going down to the pool; it was brilliant moonlight, but I couldn't get up. It was the beastliest thing that ever happened to me. We both lay there frozen, waiting for something that never happened or never came. It wasn't till half-past one that the sensation wore off and I began to feel warm again, but Charles got up and suggested spending the rest of the night in the hayloft of the barn. We did that. And the next morning, although we both felt utter fools as we said it, we agreed that nothing would persuade either of us to spend another night like that. So we bolted.'

Both of them were fairly tough, both played rugby for their respective schools, both were prefects in their respective schools, and either of them would have dished it out to any other boy fool enough to suggest that he funked anything. And both admitted to the experience without any reserve. Yet we who slept in the tent on the following night had a perfectly normal night's sleep.

The second episode took place in France during 1917.

In a quiet sector of the line, we gunners got to know pretty well the infantry we were covering. We used to keep a permanent liaison officer with Battalion HQ, and, sometimes, if our OP's were close to the front, our observing officer had the courtesy of the company mess. This is the story of a company commander in a Highland regiment and set down as he told it, without comment.

One of his subalterns was having a bad time with toothache, so an appointment was made for him with the corps' dental people who operated some distance from the line. To keep his appointment, the officer, for convenience sake let him be Jock, had to leave at the crack of dawn and was not likely to get back till after dark. Like most companies in the line, this one was short-handed, and they were expecting a new draft from the base that night. To save sending an NCO whom he could hardly spare, the company commander asked Jock to meet the new lot and guide them up the line. All of which worked out quite well.

There were two communication trenches leading into the sector they were holding. Call them Bond Street and Fetter Lane. Bond Street was the deeper, drier and better maintained. Fetter Lane, muddy, ill-drained and shallow, could not be used by day because a Hun machine-gun could and did enfilade it. By night it was sticky, unpleasant going at any time of year. Jock's instructions were to bring the draft up by Bond Street. The draft had orders to meet him at a ruined estaminet on the Arras-Bapaume road at 7 p.m. sharp.

At seven-fifteen the enemy opened up on Bond Street and gave it a plastering with heavy shell which lasted for half an hour or more. The company commander, who had already had a pretty rough day in the trenches from enemy trench mortars and lost three men, was worried about his reinforcements. As time passed he grew more worried. If the new draft had been caught in Bond Street by that shelling, they would have been sure to suffer heavily. They were overdue. And he liked to break new men in as gently as possible. So, when Jock stumbled into the dugout, he heaved a great sigh of relief. Jock reported all present and correct, and the draft handed over to the company sergeant-major. The company commander could hardly believe his ears.

'D'you mean to say you got through that strafing without a man hurt?'

'But we weren't shelled, sir. It all went down on Bond Street.'

'You came up Fetter Lane?'

'Yes, sir.'

'And a damn' good job you did. But I told you to use Bond Street.'

'I know, sir, but the colonel countermanded those orders. He told me to take 'em up the other way.'

'The colonel?'

'Yes.'

'Where did you see him?'

'At the estaminet. Just before seven.'

'Anyone with him?'

'No. Not even his orderly. I thought that a bit odd. But he called me over and told me to use Fetter Lane. Said he had a hunch about it. Seems he was right.'

The company commander reached for the whisky bottle and poured a stiff three fingers for Jock.

'Here . . . take it. You'll need this. And you can prepare for a shock.'

'Yes?'

'The colonel was killed at eleven forty-five ack emma. Major MacInnes has taken over the battalion.'

The Maiden Island lies slap in the middle of the northern outlet from Oban Bay. It is an intractable chunk of rock, an Ailsa Craig in miniature, capped with enough vegetation to satisfy the appetites of the handful of sheep that are sometimes rowed over from the mainland to graze there. Hardy sheep they are. There is nothing to see on the Maiden Island, and nothing to do unless you are a bird-watcher or care to fish from the rocks for cod or some other sea fishes with a hook and sinker. To the west lies the northernmost point of another island, Kerrera. To the east is the mainland, and on top of a steep cliff stands Dunollie Castle, a ruin of a tower and fortress which for many centuries was the home and stronghold of the MacDougall chiefs. They have since built themselves a plain, unfortified mansion among the trees to the east of their old home. At one time they were a very powerful clan in the Western Highlands and Isles, but they supported Baliol, the rival of Robert the Bruce, and lost a great part of their lands in consequence.

Like other ancient Scottish families, they have their accretion of legend, and one of these legends concerns the Maiden Island. Some time back in the thirteenth century, and that is not a long time to us Scots with the long memories, a MacDougall grew tired of his wife, doubtless for good and sufficient reasons. He misliked the idea of using violence upon her personally, so came to an arrange-ment with his butler. During his absence from home, the luckless lady of Dunollie was to be rowed across to the Maiden Island at low tide, bound to a rock and left to drown as the tide came in. The butler carried out his orders exactly. The poor lady drowned, and her cries for help went unanswered if not unheard.

Since then a legend arose that when either the chief or his heir lay in deadly peril, lights would be seen on the Maiden Island and pitiful cries would be heard.

At the dawn of the century, this present and troublesome century, MacDougall of MacDougall, a gunner officer, was fight-ing the Boers in South Africa. One very still, windless autumn night, two fishing-smacks from the island of Skye were becalmed off the Island of Lismore. They decided to get out their sweeps and row in to Oban, where they could be fairly sure of selling their catch in the morning. Rowing a fishing-smack with the long sweeps is a slow, hard and laborious business, and they did not get in till one in the morning. At daylight they reported to the harbour-master in the normal way, and, having done so, the owner of one smack asked what the trouble had been on the wee island at the mouth of the bay. From some distance out, he said, they had seen lights at the water's edge, more like torches they were than lanterns, and after the lights had gone out there were terrible cries to make the blood run cold. But when they rowed in past the island, all was quiet.

At this the harbour-master pricked up his ears. He was a local man. The fishermen, being from Skye, had no knowledge of

Argyllshire legends. But within twenty-four hours came the cable which brought the news that MacDougall of MacDougall had been killed in action.

As to the truth of this story I cannot possibly vouch. That was the form in which it was told me by Maggie, a great teller of tales, like all the Island people. It certainly made a deep impression which was nowise diminished by the daily sight of Dunollie Castle and the Maiden Island. And I never dared to ask Colonel MacDougall himself, the younger brother of the chief who died. Take it as typical of the Highland ghost story and accept it for that.

We had, of course, our local witch. Her name was Alison Learness. She had been married on a man who worked in the slate-quarries at Easdaile, but he ran away to Canada, and a good riddance by all accounts. Alison was a local woman, born Maclean.

She moved into a tumbledown cottage at the top of Glencruitten without asking anyone's leave. The laird of Glencruitten was a rich stockbroker called Shelley Bontein. Far from harassing the old woman, he set the cottage to rights for her at his own expense, and never asked a pennyworth of rent from her all the years she lived in it. He was a kind-hearted man.

As she grew older she became odd and contrary. She slept the day through and stayed up all night. She had the proper familiar for a witch in the shape of a big, sleek, black cat, the sleekest and proudest in all the county. Her clients were, for the most part, lassies who had loved too well or lassies who were not loved well enough. She cured warts by some long-range magic of her own. You told her who had the wart, where it was, paid her a shilling and, presto! two days afterwards it would drop off.

But all who wished to consult her must needs go to her by night, which suited the lassies very well indeed – in fact, that might have been the reason for her own nocturnal habits.

She became the object of much unsolicited charity. Our Oban ladies were nothing if not charitable. Their charity resembled justice in that it was not enough to be charitable, you must also be seen to be charitable. So they carried baskets through the town and told their friends, 'Just a few things for old Alison, you know.' The baskets were left on her doorstep. A pot of apple jelly, half of a chicken, the remains of the Sabbath roast or a warm shawl with no more than two or three small holes in it. There was always a note with the basket requesting its return in the near future but the baskets never were returned.

All day long the cottage stared down at the glen with blank windows, but after dark the shutters came off and there were lights inside.

I don't think the old creature wrought much evil. The local swine and cattle were never afflicted by the murrain after she had cast her eye on them. Nobody shrivelled away or suffered from mysteriously incurable diseases, nor was the Devil ever seen in her locality. But whatever her notoriety in life, it was nothing to the sensation caused by her death. Mr Bontein, who could see the lights in her windows from his study, noticed that they had not been lit for two consecutive nights, and his dairyman reported that Alison had not come for her milk. He sent his man down to see if all was well. It was not. The old woman was lying stretched out on her bed, fully clothed, her hands crossed over her bosom and stone dead. The big cat had vanished, nor was it ever seen again. When they cleaned the place up there were dozens of baskets from the charitable ladies crammed in a cupboard and more than a thousand pounds in notes and gold stuffed into the mattress she was lying on. None had the faintest idea of where it might have come from, how she had acquired it or, more important, to whom it ought to go. The charitable raged together and spoke of false pretences. Inquiries went to prove that she was alone in the world, without kith or kin. The husband had long since died in a Canadian gaol. Only one man tried to establish a claim, a namesake, Peter Maclean. But Peter happened to be the town drunkard and it was said that the only time in his life when he went voluntarily and without fighting to any police station was the time he went there to stake his claim. It was not upheld, and Alison's money went to the Crown.

No ghost having ever appeared to me, I once set out in search of an apparition. A very welcome invitation came to dine and spend the night in Stirling Castle, the depot of the Argyll and Sutherland Highlanders. No place in all Scotland, not even Edinburgh Castle, has played a greater part in Scottish history. Stirling Castle, which is also a Royal Palace, crowns a great rock rising from the lowland plains through which the stripling Forth snakes its way down to the Firth. It is like a great lion couchant staring across to the Grampians, ever watchful of the Highland rievers who slipped down to lift the Lowland cattle when they might. It also keeps an eye on the Campbell lands to the west. At the tip of its paw is the Heading Hill, the Scots equivalent of Tower Hill, where the soil has drunk the noblest blood of Scotland. It looks down on the battlefields of Stirling Bridge and Bannockburn, and every Scottish sovereign at some time or other has sheltered within its strong walls. The room I slept in had walls eleven feet thick, which made it difficult to admire a superb view to the south over the old tilting-yard. You had to hoist yourself up on the window-sill and wriggle along to the narrow slit which let in what light there was.

The object of this exercise was twofold. To dine with an old and cherished friend, and afterwards to lie in wait for the ghost of that Earl Douglas who was stabbed to the heart by his King, James II, in the course of a peace conference on the night of 22nd February 1452. The Earl's post-mortem appearances had been inventoried by an amateur of such matters, the places and times checked. The witching hour was between midnight and 1 a.m.

Having decided on our plan of action it was time to dress for dinner. It was Guest Night in the mess and the guest of honour was a visiting lieutenant-general. The mess plate gleamed among the carnations and roses on the ancient refectory table. Scarlet and yellow mess-jackets brightened the dark green and blue of the regimental tartan, miniature decorations glittered in the candle-light. The food was as good as the wine. A Guest Night with any regiment is something to remember, and this one with the Argylls was well above average.

After the pipers had marched round the table and the pipe-major had downed his ceremonial dram, handed to him by the colonel, turned about and marched out, the evening had scarcely begun. When the general left by car for Edinburgh, it was nicely on its way, and when it ended it was far too late for any self-respecting ghost, even a Douglas Earl, to be about, and it was also too late for me to have seen him if he were. Indeed, if I had seen the Douglas with a dagger in his breast, I should probably have mistaken him for a one-armed bandit.

And just a word of warning on two heads before abandoning the subject of the supernatural. If ever in Scotland you happen to see a particularly attractive little pony grazing beside a loch, don't, please don't, try to make friends with him. If you go close to him you will find, what has not been apparent before, that he has a gold bit in his mouth and a jewelled bridle. His saddle will be of scarlet leather and the stirrups of pure gold. Should this splendour tempt you to mount, you are lost. For he will take you round the loch at a canter, and when you want to dismount, you will find that you cannot. He then plunges into the loch and takes you down with him and you are seen no more by men. It is said that you have some kind of underwater existence with his earlier captures, but science has not so far confirmed that fact. The thing is a water horse. The last one seen frequented Loch Pityoulish which is near Aviemore.

And seals. You must be very careful about seals. Often as not they are not seals at all but Celtic princesses serving a kind of watery hard labour for earlier incontinence. They should neither be shot nor encouraged to follow you into the house. Though how anyone could have the heart, or rather the want of it, to shoot a seal that has popped out of the water and looked at him with what Browning in a slightly different context called its 'mild and magnificent eye' passes my understanding, and the same thing must be said of that even more enchanting creature, the otter. If shot, the seal might turn back into a princess, and that could call for a lot of explanation to the procurator fiscal, who, in Scotland, performs the functions of a coroner. The same thing might happen if you brought the live creature home. Your wife and family would be sure to ask awkward questions if a Celtic princess were to emerge from the bathroom in which you had parked a seal.

# Monsieur, Madame and Solange

MR and Mrs Shelley Bontein of Glencruitten were both confirmed heliophils who preferred to holiday in the south of France. It was there that they encountered Monsieur, and from that meeting flowered an arrangement whereby the Bonteins took over Monsieur's villa at Cannes for a whole autumn and Monsieur with his family arrived at Glencruitten to make the sport.

The first we knew of this *au pair* agreement was the arrival of a superb, white steam yacht of twelve hundred tons in Oban Bay. She first tied up at the railway pier, discharged three automobiles and a dozen servants, then cast off and dropped anchor in the middle of the bay. And there, save for one memorable excursion into the Sound of Mull, she floated all through the season for three whole months doing nothing at all and eating up a great deal of money. But we were soon to know that Monsieur could afford such little extravagances. He was enormously rich; in effect, a millionaire. To us it didn't seem quite natural. English and Scottish millionaires one accepted as one accepted the presence of Ben More. America was known to be inhabited largely by millionaires. We had heard of Rhodes, the Joels and Barnatos from South Africa, but a French millionaire was something against nature. It was strange, and a closer acquaintance with Monsieur's character soon made it seem odder still.

Shortly after the *San Salvador* came a letter to mother from Mrs Bontein asking her to call on the French family, which she promptly did, and by her excellent French won a high place in the regard of Madame.

The family arrived by train. Monsieur, although he was a passionate believer in 'the done thing', never believed in over-doing it. He kept a yacht because it was an appurtenance proper to one in his position. International financiers of that era kept yachts. He went so far as to entertain on board her in Mediterranean harbours, but the thought of actually going to sea in her never crossed his mind. In his view, that would have been overdoing it.

Monsieur was short, well rounded and most formidably mous-tached. In the illustrated version of 'King Solomon's Mines' there was a picture of Alphonse, a French cook, who was foolish enough to annoy Umslopagaas and for that reason had his mus-tachios shorn off by that terrible Zulu's terrible axe. The artist's conception of Alphonse could very well have been modelled by Monsieur. Anyhow, they were inseparable in my mind's eye. Madame resembled her husband, also being short, well rounded and somewhat moustached. Both were dark, excitable and agonis-ingly curious. Monsieur dared to ask Lady Breadalbane over the luncheon-table just how many millions were at the disposal of M. le Marquis. He did not do so twice.

Both Madame and her husband shared a virtue which, in my experience, is not generally characteristic of their country. They were both wildly and extravagantly hospitable on a scale which rather took us aback. You could not be ten minutes in a room with Madame, no matter what the hour, without finding something to eat or to drink at your side, and when Monsieur signalled '*A boire!*' to his butler, a veritable forest of exotically shaped bottles filled with liquids of every colour in the spectrum would be wheeled in on a two-tiered trolley. When Madame received our Argyllshire ladies for tea, Monsieur would embarrass them with encouragements to abandon their tea and take liqueurs instead. Madame herself sipped little glasses of 'porto', the only thing she touched away from the dinner-table. In hot weather she took it frappé, at all kinds of hours.

This habit rather horrified some of her less travelled guests, and inadvertently led one of them to drop a brick of the first magnitude. He was a retired soldier with a jolly wife whose golden tresses were admired by all men and suspected by all women. They were a devoted pair who rented a small estate which marched with Glencruitten. The major was a conventional type, much liked for his good nature but not highly fancied for the intelligence stakes. Offered 'porto' at tea-time, and with cracked ice at that, he began to brood over it. It made it all the worse that the label on the bottle bore the classic name of Cockburn and the year . . . well, it was one of the classic years. It was something quite outside the range of his experience. He had a palate and a deep reverence for the ritual associated with the wine. When they left Glencruitten House one evening, his wife went straight home, but he slipped into Oban to collect a parcel from the railway station. Having collected it, he dropped into the Station Hotel for a dram and there unbosomed himself to the barman and two or three acquaintances. 'Vintage port with tea . . . and ice in the glass . . . 'strordinary games these foreign fellers – their wives I ought to say – get up to!' His dram and his story were thrice repeated before he decided to go home and he marched out of the hotel leaving his parcel on the bar. Someone spotted it in time and went after him. The major was effusively grateful.

'Very kind of you, m'dear feller. Very kind of you indeed. Never have done to forget that . . . m'wife's hair, as a matter fact. Chap in Princes Street touches it up for her . . . dinin' out tonight, too . . . never have done to forget that.'

How two such improbable parents as Monsieur and Madame contrived to compound a daughter like Solange will always be a profound mystery. Solange, in contemporary idiom, was a dish, a wow, a humdinger, a smasher and a pin-up. More than that. For one short season she shook the thrones of established beauties, subverted their liegemen and would have done so no less surely had she not been sole heiress to Monsieur's millions. Solange had assets of her own in the form of soft chestnut hair which owed nothing to adventitious aid, dark-blue eyes, a mouth perhaps a shade too wide for her heart-shaped face, perfect teeth, a clear, velvety complexion and statistics which were no less vital than her gay, frank and lively personality. She was in her nineteenth year, spoke fluent, idiomatic English as well as German, Italian and Spanish. Her golf was good enough for any company short of the very best, her tennis better than her golf, and she was the first young girl to drive her own car round the county unchaperoned. Few French parents, and not many British ones for that matter, would have allowed a '*jeune fille*' the freedom Solange took for granted. The occasion when Campbell Muir bunted her and her car into Loch Awe and then swore at her for getting in his way took place early in her visit, I had almost written 'reign', and perhaps aroused in her certain misgivings regarding the local *jeunesse dorée*.

Being three years younger than Solange, I was going through the painful period when a boy's susceptibility is only surpassed by his determination to conceal it, and it was a devastating experience to be exposed at close quarters to anyone like Solange. Mrs Bontein's letter and mother's prompt response gave me an appreciable lead over my contemporaries, but it was not till considerably later that I came to see how useful she found me. Besieged by Allans and Alastairs, Duncans and Donalds, Ians and Torquils, Solange nevertheless insisted on having me about on all possible occasions. What one almost dared to hope might have been a slight *tendresse* was no more than a form of insurance against the greater enterprise of the Allans and Alastairs aforesaid. Sentimental episodes between us just did not occur; Solange saw to that. But that was a golden summer and we filled it with golf and tennis, picnics and bathing, impromptu suppers and dances, and the Twelfth was upon us in no time at all.

Monsieur's ostensible reason for coming to Argyll was to make the sport. What one feels he really wanted was to be able to say casually to his fellow-members of some Parisian *cercle* that he had taken a shoot in Scotland that year, and probably enjoy at the same time a rich man's satisfaction that it had cost him very little. For all I know, he may have been a pioneer. French shooting-tenants were then very rare birds indeed. Spanish kings, German serene highnesses, Austrian counts, Polish princes, Sassoons and Rothschilds were no strangers to the Highlands, but Frenchmen were scarce. The French sportsman was looked upon as a kind of joke, an illusion fostered by *Punch*, which printed drawings of a French count aiming at a running pheasant while his loader says 'No, no, Mounseer, we don't shoot at running birds!' and the count replies, '*Zut alors!* I vait teel he stop!'

For all his determination to shoot, Monsieur never both-ered his head about organising a shoot. Then it was far too late. Glencruitten was not a very good moor. When Mr Bontein was at home he and perhaps three other guns would walk up their birds over dogs and feel quite happy with a dozen or fifteen brace. The place was never driven, at least not at that time. The keeper was an ancient old man long past his best. Mr Bontein had an endearing kindness for the old, who continued in his service long after more exacting masters would have pensioned them off. If my father, who was spending his Twelfth in Inverness-shire, had not chanced to ask Monsieur about his arrangements, there would have been no arrangements at all. As it was, they were of the most sketchy. Monsieur disliked to admit ignorance of any kind – perhaps it is a foible of the rich – but having taken in the fact that dogs would be needed, he ceased to listen. Dogs, he said, would be forthcoming. He would see to that. But guns presented an insu-perable obstacle. Having neglected to invite any, it was then too late, since everyone, even the most devoted of Solange's admirers, was already booked up. Not liking the thought of our friends, and they were that already, being turned loose without any experi-enced person to help them, father did the best he could, which consisted in cancelling my visit to Glenfeochan and attaching me, far from unwilling, to the Glencruitten party. It was, he said, better than nothing. Solange he had already taken in hand and taught to hit clay pigeons, with my sixteen-bore, and, needless to say, she did it very well. Of her father's experience, beyond the fact that he had shot in France, she could tell us nothing. Monsieur himself seemed to be more interested in discovering the proper ceremonial for the occasion than in the shoot itself, and he was rather disappointed to find that there were no traditional fan-fares and no precedent for the employment of, say, a pipe band, when marching out to make the sport.

So it came about that on the morning of the tenth, Solange and I could have been seen standing beneath the great wire baskets of pink geraniums with which our stationmaster, Mr MacPhee, embellished the platforms, waiting for the London train. With us was the ancient keeper, Farquhar Coll, who had driven down in a dog-cart which, for once, would fulfil the proper function of a dog-cart and carry Monsieur's dogs from the station to Glencruitten kennels. I don't know whether old Farquhar or I was the more astonished when the guard's van yielded up two couple of bitch fox-hounds. Monsieur, or his London agent, had made a mistake. The bitches had a sensational social success. Never before had foxhounds been seen in Oban station. English visitors who knew what they were looking at made much of them, as did all the children in the place, and by noon Oban was speculating on what esoteric uses they might be put to. It was a job to get them in the dog-cart. They were driven to the house, spent a night in the kennels, and returned to their proper employments on the following day.

Deprived of ceremony, Monsieur insisted on a '*déjeuner de chasse*'. It was a peculiar meal and the first time I was ever called upon to drink champagne at breakfast. Monsieur appeared in a green corduroy coat with the rosette of the Legion in its buttonhole. He was never seen without his rosette. Unkind people said that he wore it on his pyjamas, but that canard was never confirmed and, anyhow, Monsieur was more the type to favour a nightgown. Below his green coat were striped business trousers almost totally concealed by long, soft leather gaiters which buttoned up the side and were strapped to a belt like salmon-waders. When we started out, a Tyrolean hat was added to this kit, a gun with a leather sling hung from one shoulder, and a large and hopeful-looking game-bag from the other. All the staff, butler, chef, three footmen, *valet de chambre* and maids galore were assembled outside the front door, and there was a great shaking of hands and Madame embraced everybody. Perhaps there *ought* to have been two *chasseurs* with curly horns in the background, but there were not. At last we started off. There was a short half-mile to walk through pine-woods and along the edge of a cornfield where we fell into Indian file led by Coll, followed by Solange, by me and by Monsieur in that order. As it had long been dinned into me that no gun should be carried loaded before you reach the place where you expect to use it, mine was empty when two wood-pigeons rose from the corn on our right. There was a colossal bang – it seemed to be right behind my ear – followed by a second in quick succession. The pigeons flew happily on and Monsieur broke his gun, ejected the empty cases, blew down the barrels and said to Solange, 'It is enough! I return. Good hunting!' Whereupon he strolled back, waving a plump hand, leaving Solange and me with Coll, a fat old retriever, and the whole of the Twelfth before us. As I have tried to point out, Monsieur did not believe in excess. He had discharged his gun on the Twelfth of August, if not on, at least on the verge of his moor. It sufficed.

What sort of reception committee welcomed him back, I do not know. During the rest of the day, except when we were eating a superb picnic lunch served by a footman apiece, Solange and I walked and worked hard for our eight and a half brace and, at the end of the day, felt that we had earned them. Monsieur never went out again. Solange tried hard to persuade him that he owed it to himself to shoot at least one *coq de bruyère*, but Monsieur thought otherwise, although he very much appreciated roast grouse cooked in the Highland fashion. My father also taught him to appreciate whisky and differentiate between a fine old malt and the lesser blends he had met hitherto.

To say that Solange was a success at the year's Gathering balls would be one of the understatements of all time. What follows is hearsay, as I was then considered too young for such doings. The Ians and Torquils, the Duncans and Donalds, for all their Highland splendour, did not have it all their own way by any means. The Navy was there to offer a little competition. The Beauties disliked it intensely. One of them, and it must have been a new experience for her, was actually without a partner for a whole dance while the gentleman who owned the name on her programme waltzed in a kind of happy trance with Solange. Remote as we were from the great world and the smart set, not all of our girls were without jealousy.

'Hamish chasing after that foreign creature! What fools men make of themselves.'

'If you ask *me*, I think she's *fast*.'

'After all, she's only a tradesman's daughter.'

It had become known that part of Monsieur's revenues were derived from his ownership of the Bon Marché in Paris.

'And that frock . . . Poiret they say. Much too sophisticated for a gel of that age.'

'Dessay even we might afford Poiret at trade rates.'

All of which, and she heard some of it as she was doubtless intended to, was so much water off a duck's back. Solange was enjoying herself and so were her partners, for she danced as well as she did everything else.

Solange, like the rest of the family, took neither pleasure nor interest – at least none of them gave any indication of doing so – in the great yacht, the largest in the bay and a focus of general attention. That Monsieur and Madame were content to make a kind of status symbol of that lovely thing was perhaps comprehensible. They were no longer young and perhaps they were bad sailors. But Solange was a good sailor and enjoyed tacking about the bay in a sailing-boat. Even during the regattas, when most owners of large craft gave parties on board, neither Monsieur or Madame, those most hospitable of people, did anything about it.

Like the other yachts, only rather more so, the *San Salvador* was dressed with bunting and illuminated at night. She made too, a substantial contribution to the fireworks which always signalled the end of the season. Although we had known the family ever since they came and had exchanged dinners, luncheons and parties of one kind or another almost every week, it had never seemed to occur to any of them that we could be intensely interested in the *San Salvador* herself. So when a card arrived for a PPC party on board, to take the form of an afternoon cruise in the Sound of Mull, I don't think anyone in Argyllshire who received the invitation refused it. The idea was Solange's. It had, as Madame told us, been very carefully explained to Monsieur that the yacht would be in sheltered waters all the way and that there would be no question of going to sea.

The day, when it came, could hardly have been more propitious. It was bright and sunny with no more than the lightest of breezes, and it stayed that way to the last. The guests assembled at two different jetties, whence they were taken off by the yacht's steam-launches. There were two of them. Most of the fleet had already weighed anchor, but HMS *Colossus* was still there to send a quota of naval leaven to lighten the party. At first everybody was too interested in the yacht herself to pay much attention to their fellow guests, and it was not till we were under way and passing through the narrows between Kerrera and the Maiden Island that the parade-ground voice of a heavily landed laird was heard to rumble to his wife, 'But good God, Amy . . . isn't that the feller y' get y'r bacon from?'

It was. Not only were Mr and Mrs Grocer of the party, but Mr and Mrs Baker, Mr and Mrs and the little Garages, Mr and Mrs Fishmonger and their shoal of bairns . . . in fact, all the tradesfolk who had supplied Glencruitten since the arrival of Monsieur, Madame and Solange.

Today, such a mixture would hardly raise an eyebrow. But then it was very, very different. Nor was it like a garden-party, where escape was possible for those who worried about their social chastity. Short of diving over the side there was no escape. There were the County and Trade, both rubbing shoulders, however little they liked it, for two whole hours. What else could you expect from foreigners? That some of the County owed some of the tradesmen rather more for rather longer than they should have, didn't help to ease the initial awkwardness. But Monsieur's stewards were soon on the job with glasses of champagne and sandwiches, and champagne is undoubtedly the best of all social lubricants. The men of both parties fell upon it, part to the manner born, part experimentally. After a glass or two one didn't wonder what one's wife would have to say later; after three or four, who cared? A great deal of what is described as snobbery in these islands is really no more than shyness.

The ladies, by convention denied such solvents, at least quantitively, although some of the elder ones made good use of it, found another catalyst. The blessed catalyst of children; for it is just not possible for decent folk, and most of them were just that, to be stand-offish with bairns under their feet.

The imperfect comprehension of English by our host and hostess, further bedevilled by Lowland and Highland accents, threw them back on the ultimate resource of hospitality . . . another glass of champagne? It wasn't often refused. By the time the Lismore lighthouse fell astern, the party was growing lively, although there was a tendency for the males to conglobulate, if one may borrow from the great Doctor. Monsieur and Madame, with typically French distrust of *courants d'air*, held court in the saloon. Most of their guests preferred the deck.

Gradually the excursion turned into a roaring success.

It was discovered that Mr Grocer who retailed such excellent Ayrshire bacon could also relate a fund of pungent West Highland stories and that Mr Fishmonger naturally knew all about the wonders of the deep we were sailing over. In fact, by the time we put about and headed for Oban Bay again, most present had revealed themselves to each other as human beings rather than representatives of different classes. Solange, with a willing staff of

*Colossus* officers, looked after the deck-party, and the Navy did its full share in producing the general well-being that prevailed when we dropped anchor again. It was quite a party.

But not for me. It marked the end of a glorious holiday. And Solange, who had been my sun, moon and stars for nearly three months, was going home. Tomorrow the cars would be re-embarked on the *San Salvador*, the staff would go aboard, and our French friends leave on the London train. When you are young it is hard to understand that things must come to an end, especially when, for the first time, you are not a little in love. It was years afterwards when it struck me that Solange's improbable party might possibly have been her revenge for certain remarks passed at the Gathering ball. Good republicans, the family never showed undue respect for rank, and Monsieur's reverence was certainly monopolised by the Golden Calf. Nevertheless . . .

Solange went back to France and stayed there. We were to meet again in Paris for a few moments sometime after the Armistice of 1918. The King, with the Prince of Wales and Duke of York, paid a visit to the French capital, *en garçon*, and Lord Derby held a big reception for them at the Embassy. I happened to be on leave with father and mother: his headquarters were in Paris at that time. I was very anxious to see the great French generals of the war, Foch in particular. To most of us in the BEF they were no more than names. So it was arranged that my father's card should also cover my arrival at the function. It was a most interesting evening. The almost universal appearance of service dress rather took the glitter away, but some of the ladies present did their best to make up for it. After the Royal party withdrew, the young Princes disappeared fairly early but the King stayed on. We went to the buffet to quench a thirst begotten of overheated salons, the press of humanity and standing on one's feet for a long time. And there at the buffet was Solange, with her husband. A Solange even more attractive and beautiful than ever. She had two sons, she said. It seemed that she had not so much married as contracted an alliance. The very noble family whose name and titles she bore had no need of her money. Her husband was a distinguished historian and philologist, a rich landowner and a Member of the Académie Française. Madame, alas, had died in 1916. Monsieur was still much occupied with affairs, and had been awarded the plaque of the Legion for his war services to his own country and a CBE from us. 'He still drinks his whisky,' Solange said to father. 'You taught him that!' So Monsieur did take something back to France with him from Argyllshire.

There is an amusing little story about the family Solange married into. The founder of the house was granted his lands for service on Crusade to St Louis of France. This worthy knight also brought home a wife from the Holy Land. She was a Jewish lady, a Levite, to which tribe also belonged Mary the Mother of Jesus.

In Bourbon times the distinction of being called 'cousin' by the King of France was much sought after, and many families paid large sums to professional genealogists in hopes of establishing a right to that honour. Not so the family of Solange's husband. In the hall of their château – it lies near Foix – they have a very ancient, life-size, wooden carving of the Madonna and child. It is of Spanish origin and dates from the thirteenth century. The carving stands by the foot of the grand staircase in the hall of the château. It is much admired by artists; good Catholics bow or genuflect to it when passing by. But the owner of the château is content to nod cheerfully in its direction and say '*Bon jour*' or perhaps '*Bon soir . . . ma cousine!*'

They never considered that a cousin of the Mother of God need exert himself to claim kinship to a mere King of France.

# Envoi – Some Comparisons

In many respects the small boy of today is better off than we used to be. To generalise, he has more and much better toys than we ever hoped for; the family car gives him a range and scope we never dreamed of; he has more pocket-money and more objects to spend it on. He seems, at least whenever I encounter him, to eat between meals without restriction, and his clothes are practical, comfortable and more attractive. He never suffers from 'Sunday best'. Obviously his health is excellent and his manners leave little to be desired. Of his education I cannot speak, but it seems less Spartan, more eclectic and no longer rammed into his head quite so relentlessly as before. Yet I have seen nothing that might make me wish to change places with him.

If we were more disciplined, we were, paradoxically, much more free. There were laws of the Medes and Persians which might never be broken with impunity. Punctuality at mealtimes for instance. One just didn't accept the casual invitation to lunch after a game of golf; never before the telephone was installed, and not often then. Breakfast at 9, luncheon at 1.30, dinner at 8.15, and you changed for dinner. Not necessarily into a boiled shirt unless there were guests, but change you did. Afternoon tea alone was excepted and might be missed without due warning. To be late for breakfast was forgivable provided one had gone out before breakfast. What was called 'fugging in bed' got very different treatment. But there was little or no difficulty about going off on your own, here, there or anywhere, 'so long as we know where you are' and provided you had enough money for your needs. You seldom had. Pocket-money was at the rate of two shillings a week during holiday times. For any special excursion, you presented an estimate of outlay. As a matter of principle, the sum asked was always reduced, so one learned to make plausible over-estimates to meet that contingency.

Mother, when a young girl, was once stranded, penniless, in Berlin when those who should have met her were involved in a railway accident. Sensibly, she went to the embassy for help, which was given without undue difficulty. But ever after she had a horror of anyone in the family being so placed. For me she devised an emergency fund in a characteristic way. Whenever a new jacket came from the tailor, a gold sovereign was stitched into the inside breast-pocket. This was only to be spent if there was real need. If spent, a report had to be made, and if the need was approved, the coin was replaced. As things were then, there were very few places in Scotland, let alone Argyll, from whence one could not travel home for less than twenty shillings. The presence of this hoard in my clothing was checked at the beginning of each holiday. (By an irony of fate, the only time a justifiable emergency did arise, I was in shirt-sleeves and without a jacket.) On embarkation leave before I sailed for Gallipoli, we went through my old clothes and extracted five sovereigns. To those I added fifteen more and carried them in a belt on the same emergency principle. They were never spent, and I know today where they could be found . . . at the bottom of Mudros Bay, together with a sword . . . yes, we took swords to Gallipoli . . . a pair of Zeiss binoculars, a .45 Webley and a prismatic compass. They were dropped into the water between the launch that took me off to a hospital ship and the ship's companionway. They went down as I crept up the ladder, a yellow skeleton, thanks to the combined operation of jaundice and dysentery, and too feeble to curse the idiot who dropped them.

From a boy's point of view, the Oban house had one draw-back. The road up from town was so steep as to make bicycling impractical. One would have had to push all the way home. So I never learned how to bicycle. But even that disadvantage turned to benefit. There was always a pony in the stable. One's friends might be able to go farther by road, but a pony freed one from roads of any kind. The Highland garron is a sturdy, biddable beast, dun-coloured with a black stripe down its back and gifted with a sixth sense when it comes to avoiding bog and marshy ground in rough moorland country. If you happened to be away for a night, there was never any difficulty about finding accommodation. Today it may be harder. It has always surprised me that the pony-trekking holiday took so long to develop in the Highlands. There is no better way of enjoying the hills and learning topography than from the back of a garron.

Given a pony, a rod and a gun, together with ample opportunity for using all three; given the opportunity of 'messing about in small boats' whenever he felt like it, and all the golf and tennis he could make time for, no boy had cause for complaint nor any excuse for boredom.

There was also the illegal excitement of occasional poaching forays. And all this in some of the loveliest country in all Scotland among its kindliest and most hospitable people. Not many boys of today have that kind of luck. If the crofter is less welcoming to the hiker and bicyclist of today, it is only because the town-bred are too free with their matches, too off-hand in their manner, and not careful enough with their litter. Cellophane is an admirable wrapping, but it does not eventually dissolve in the rain like paper and blows about till it must be collected and destroyed.

At the beginning of the century any boy on a pony could find sweet hay to sleep on, shelter for his beast if necessary, and strong tea, fresh eggs, soda scones with home-made jam, butter and cream, perhaps kebbuck cheese, at almost any croft or farmhouse he cared to call at anywhere in the county. And no native-born would be stupid or tactless enough to offer payment, Highland hospitality being what it was. Such kindness would be acknowledged by a gift at Christmastide and a careful record was kept of all such obligations.

# Envoi – Some Comparisons

If it is otherwise today, well, circumstances alter cases, and the whole art of housekeeping seems to have undergone quite a radical change. In a country house of any size, the housewife bought her stores in bulk and always had enough on hand to deal with any emergency. Each house had its store-room, of which the mistress kept the key as her husband kept the key of the cellar. It all followed a clear-cut, well-understood pattern.

On Monday there was the conference with Mrs O'Callaghan at which the menus for the week were roughed out. She would then decide what was needful in the way of flour, butter, eggs, oatmeal, jam, bacon and cheese. A procession of household staff, each armed with various receptacles, followed mother upstairs, the store-room was unlocked, the scales put on the table, and the various stuffs weighed out and taken downstairs. The store-room was worth seeing, and raiding sometimes. There were farm-cured bacon and hams, sacks of flour, oatmeal and sugar; pots and pots of home-made jam and marmalade. One wall was shelved, the boards perforated to take dozens of preserved eggs for cooking purposes . . . and there were more exotic supplies like cherries and angelica, curry powders and poppadums and Bombay duck, sticks of cinnamon (sometimes sneaked to smoke: they weren't a success, they never drew properly), tins of Bath Olivers, whole cheeses, stem ginger and Elvas plums.

The exotic delights came from The Army and Navy Co-operative Society, known as the Army and Navy, *tout court*. We were members of that august institution, and its catalogue played quite a part in our lives. It was a huge tome, some two thousand pages, bound in scarlet and 'profusely illustrated'. On cold, wet, blustery days, the 'Army and Navy' was studied from cover to cover on the nursery floor. It was fascinating, mouth-watering reading. You could find anything. Clockwork, self-propelled scale models of battleships at 66/6d. There was nothing you could not get from the Army and Navy. Father got his wine, cigars and cigarettes from them. Not even our local ironmonger, Mr Munro, whose proud slogan was 'From a trout fly to a steam yacht', could compare with the Army and Navy. Mr Munro's advertising was perfectly true, all the same. It was before advertising got bedevilled with psychology and attempted to erect itself into a learned profession. The Army and Navy offered a yard-stick for prices. You could see just how much you were being over-charged locally for almost any commodity. Ladies would call for 'just a peep at the "Army and Navy".' It was never lent out. However, as local tradesmen improved, the Army and Navy did less business with us every year, till they ceased to do any at all; wines, cigars and cigarettes excepted.

Fish was cheap, plentiful and fresh from the sea. Vegetables, potatoes included, came from the garden, each in its own season, and there were ample supplies of fruit. We had our own poultry yard. In such circumstances the unexpected arrival of four or five guests never presented much of a problem. The last-minute rush for a (tasteless) frozen chicken and some (savourless) frozen peas was unknown. Housekeeping, in fact, ran from quarter day to quarter day and not from week to week. We knew where our flour was grown and milled, we knew the farm our oatmeal came from, and, although we never kept a cow, the milk, cream and butter was provided by certain Jersey and Ayrshire ladies who pastured by the lodge gates and were familiar friends. The 'pig in a pretty poke' system of retailing, which compels the customer to do the assistant's work for him, never allows him to see what he is getting, and tries to persuade the customer that he, not the vendor, is the beneficiary, had not been born. Nor had the battling cereals which fight for your custom on TV and hoarding. Porridge was the only cereal we knew. Porridge made from coarse oatmeal, salted and eaten with cream . . . and always eaten standing up. Sugar and syrup were to be had for weak brethren and Sassenachs, but such effeminacy was looked at sideways. My grandmother still spoke of porridge as 'them', not 'it'. That was the old-fashioned way of referring to it, and I have not heard it used since her death.

Does age dull the palate? None of the judges of wine I have known were young men, but one can't help feeling that however sanitary and attractive modern packaging has become, the stuff inside the package has lost some of its savour. There is one notable exception to this generalisation. Beef is better than it ever was, frozen or chilled beef being excepted.

My generation seemed to spend more time out of doors than my young friends do now, and we were less troubled by bad weather. Of course it must be admitted that nobody who suffers from an allergy to rain could possibly enjoy life in the West Highlands, say the travel posters what they may. It does rain. But we didn't necessarily regard wet weather as bad weather. Fishermen don't. To us it was not the calamity that sent the England players back to the pavilion or spoiled the tennis tournament. Rain meant spate and, spate subsiding, rain meant baskets of brown trout taken on a worm. We took rain in our stride, indeed we wouldn't have got very far had we not done so. We played golf in the rain and thought nothing of it. Rain, like whisky, was part of our birthright, and when you grew up you learned that the one offset the other. West Highland rain is soft and warm for the most part, and never hurts anyone who has the sense to change as soon as he gets indoors. One had to go to the effeminate Lowlands before anyone ever made a fuss about wet feet. Broadly speaking, outdoor attractions won hands down over anything that indoors could provide, but of course we didn't have a chance to see the England–Scotland rugby game at Inverleith (Murrayfield was not born in those days) on TV And we never had the variety and excellence of modern rain and windproof materials either.

Natural history was part of our everyday life. There was no setting out to learn it. It came in conversation and observation. John MacKechnie, the gardener, who could just sign his name with some difficulty and effort, knew more about the habits of beast and bird than many a professed naturalist. If John remarked that he thought the woodcock would be in on Friday night, you could bet your last halfpenny that the birds would be there on Saturday morning. John loved all birds, in spite of their depredations in his garden, and woebetide any lad he caught bird-nesting in the woods. He cured me of egg-collecting once and for all – and which, all said and done, would you prefer . . . a goldfinch's egg-shell on cotton-wool in a box with a Latin label . . . or another family of finches in the wood? Egg collectors are intemperate folk, witness the story of the ospreys at Loch Garten in Strathspey and the measures needed to protect them. Let the collectors satisfy themselves with photographs now that colour pictures are easy and cheap. Many a big-game hunter has made the change.

All this pouring out of words brings to mind another rule that was strictly observed. In the society of your elders, you just didn't speak till you were spoken to. If at times you were not far short of bursting, you did learn to listen, and good listeners are few and far between. The rule was most rigidly applied at table. When broken, you were sent out of the room and lost the rest of your meal, most likely the pudding. That is if you didn't have friends in the kitchen. Judging by the happy babel which prevails round family tables today, it is no longer enforced. Nor, I think, would it have been with us unless it were known that the kitchen would never let a boy go hungry if they could help it.

Only one occasion ever arose when I questioned the parental justice. Coming home from prep school by train on the Callander and Oban Railway, a line known by heart and still loved, the Devil suggested that it might be fun to dodge the ticket-collector and arrive home with a ticket unpunched. It was easy. One knew at which stations the collectors came round, and the lavatory was handy. That night, the first night of the summer holidays, the ticket was produced, intact, and put on the table. It seemed to be quite a harmless joke; after all, the ticket had been paid for. But no. Thunder clouds gathered and the lightning of reprisals struck. It was dishonest. Dishonesty was right up at the top of the criminal code. Condign punishment ensued and I went sore to bed. Not only that. Next day I was sent to the station to hand the ticket over to Mr MacPhee the stationmaster, apologise, and submit to any penalty he thought fit to impose. This was duly done. The genial and rubicund Mr MacPhee, who most certainly had been briefed in advance, did his best to appear forbidding, without much success. He read me a lecture on deceit and the awful consequences of deceit, and ended it up by saying that on this one occasion the Callander and Oban Railway Company would take no action. But if it happened again . . . terrible penalties would be exacted. Then he spoiled it all. I was no sooner outside his door when I heard him roaring with laughter and . . . 'The wee deevil . . . whoever would be thinking that he would try such a thing!'

That was the end of the matter, for in our house punishment carried absolution with it, and crimes were never brought up a second time or even mentioned. Probably the fact that my father was a director of the line made him unduly conscious of this prank. He was always most scrupulous about our not receiving special treatment from the railway . . . almost as careful as the railway were to see that we did. He little knew that when there was nothing better to do, one would travel up to Connel Ferry on the foot-plate and return with the engine-driver on the afternoon train from Glasgow. There was another privilege, much cherished and appreciated. On the way back to school one would be seen off at Oban in the proper third-class carriage. At Connel Ferry, by Mr MacPhee's instructions, the guard would come and beckon. I would then be taken to the very end of the train and locked into a first-class coupé, if, of course, it had not been reserved. That made one's day and took the curse off the first night at school. These coupés, you don't see them any more, consisted of two seats with a lavatory door between them and a window opposite each seat.

You sat with your back to the engine and watched the countryside fall away behind you. It seemed to lend a special thrill to travelling, especially when you knew that nobody else in the whole train could see that ever wonderful panorama of loch and mountain in just the same way. After the affair of the ticket, such matters were strictly between Mr MacPhee, the guard and me.

There was one thing the little Callander and Oban could do which the mighty British Railways cannot. The line was not long enough to warrant dining-cars. You could, however, telegraph for a luncheon-basket which was handed in at Callander. The contents were always exactly the same. Half a cold roast chicken, half a bottle of claret, salad, cheese, biscuits, butter, a roll, an apple and a paper screw of salt in the bottom of a tumbler. It cost half a crown.

Experience has taught me that if you wish to lead a pleasant and satisfactory life, you should pitch your tent where the tempo of life is slow. It is even more important than finding a beautiful camping-ground. In Argyllshire both these desirable conditions were present. As a Shetlander recently said to my wife, 'Up here, we have time to live.' The West Highland tempo used to be slow. Slow enough for the courtesies of life, and few matters were ever urgent enough to demand immediate action. That meant that there was time for thought before action. That, I suspect, is probably why the West Highlander had a reputation for laziness which he has never truly deserved. His life was a hard, constant struggle against barren soil and high seas, with seldom sufficient resources with which to face unexpected calamity. In Victorian days there was a trick of referring to the crofter, the gillie or the fisherman as 'nature's gentlemen'. A beastly, patronising phrase it is too. Those who used it never dreamed that those they referred to were, likely as not, in the heraldic sense, gentlemen of coat armour. If the Irish mostly claim descent from kings of the Emerald Isle, most men of Argyll could claim kinship with their chiefs, did they but know their own pedigrees. Before pen and ink came into general use, the first thing taught to a Highland lad was his pedigree, and he was expected to have it by heart for transmission to his own family in turn. In the days of clan warfare it was always wise to know whether you had blood kin on the enemy side.

These pedigrees were seldom, if ever, set down on paper, and that which is called aristocracy depends more than anything else on the possession of written records of your forefathers.

Parchment and seals took a long time to penetrate the Highlands, whose chiefs resisted the feudal system as long as they could do so in safety. In some intellectual circles today the word 'gentleman' is almost a dirty word. Yet one may think of a Socialist acquaintance in this connection. He despises birth, breeding and hereditary titles of every kind and says so on every possible occasion. But this same scoffer thinks nothing of spending two hours in deep study of the blood lines of each runner in the 3.30 at Lingfield before he puts on his dollar or half-dollar as the case may be. It is not altogether logical. So I go further than the Victorian in this matter and assert gladly that the Highlander is a gentleman and a very fine gentleman too.

In all sincerity he wishes nothing better than to live at amity with all men. It is an attitude which begets a positive loathing of discourtesy, and any supposed slight rankles in a memory little inferior to that of the elephant. In civil life, he makes the best of friends but a bad enemy. His record in war speaks for itself. Lowlanders were all too ready to regard him as 'simple' and lazy. He can be a rogue, and those who come upon him for the first time are often deluded into the belief that he has no sense of humour. They could hardly be more wrong. The Highlander can look you in the eye with a grave face while, inwardly, he is shaking with laughter.

As an example, John Buchanan springs to mind. That was not his name but t'will serve. He was first a fisherman, but in middle age took to running a ferry between his own island and the mainland. John was a large, brown-bearded, genial man with the gift of making his passenger feel safe with him in any kind of weather. Indeed, he would assure them with complete truth that he had never lost a passenger or a parcel in the whole of his life. He had one very noticeable idiosyncrasy. Wet or fine, whatever the weather, he always wore a battered top hat. The hat, in a way, became a feature of the place. John apart, only the minister possessed such a thing. Visitors asked for the ferryman with the top hat and felt abused if they did not see him. Everybody made jokes about it and all the jokes were taken in good part. He was heard to say that he had developed a superstition about the hat, and if he were ever to lose it overboard, he would never cross the ferry any more. John never capitalised his celebrity and popularity by drinking at the expense of tourists who were all too ready to buy him drams. He was a very, very moderate drinker, and was frequently held up as an example to those who were not. He lived alone, for he was a widower, in a cottage by the shore, which was kept as clean, if not cleaner, than any woman could have kept it.

But time rolled on and there came a morning when John failed to answer the signal for the ferry. The policeman went to investigate and, alas, found John, old John he was by then, neatly dead in his bed with his grizzled beard spread out over the white counterpane. The famous top hat lay on the floor by the bedside. When the policeman, not without reverence for so famed an object, picked it up, it seemed to be rather heavy. And no wonder. The upper part of the hat contained a small tin cistern filled with rather more than a pint of very newly distilled whisky. When the local statisticians got to work on the average number of trips per day multiplied by 365, for he was on call on Sabbath days as well as week-days, multiplied again by the years he had worn the hat, it was soon apparent that John, even at the then prevailing rates of duty, must have been heavily in debt to the Inland Revenue, and had handled enough of the stuff to float, if not a battleship, at least a destroyer. John himself was long buried before they found out that there was not one top hat but two top hats, and each time John crossed over he left the empty hat in a certain privy where his distilling friends on the mainland took good care that he should find a full one.

John was a very typical West Highlander. He was never in a hurry. He was modest about quantities. It is easy to see how he must have enjoyed ferrying the police across, with whom he was on the best possible terms, to say nothing of the Inland Revenue officers with whom, in those days, few Highlanders cared to associate. But unless I am very, very wrong, his deepest satisfaction came from outwitting the Government day after day under the very noses of their accredited representatives without ever arousing the least breath of suspicion. He knew well that nothing was less likely to succeed than excess. And you must remember that ever since the aftermath of Culloden, 'the Government' has been a suspect phrase in the Highlands. Too many evil memories of attempted genocide, transportations, confiscations, hangings and burnings and, even worse, neglect, were associated with it.

No born West Highlander could regard John as a reprehensible character. There is, I have been told, a fine Gaelic poem which celebrates his achievement.

Oban used to call herself 'The Charing Cross of the Highlands'. The tourist trade makes a misnomer out of that. In summer she is more like Piccadilly Circus. The quality have yielded place to the quantity. Buses by the dozen disgorge their loads of trippers all through the season; American cruising liners loose their hundreds of passengers; cars swarm past the flanks of Cruachan and through the Pass of Brander heading to Oban, all summer long. The tempo is changing. But much remains. The incomparable view over the bay, over Kerrera and the Dutchman's Hat, over the Sound to Mull and Ben More: nothing can spoil that. The green island of Lismore, supposed by some to be the earliest haven of Christianity in Scotland, points its long finger down a blue Loch Linnhe with its twinkling, terminal lighthouse by the Sound of Mull. Dunollie Castle dozes over the bay's mouth, more like a retired general in a club chair than the once alert sentinel of MacDougall power.

The past is still there for those with eyes to see and ears to hear, and the present buys Iona stone souvenirs, china souvenirs with the arms of the burgh, toy bagpipes in Campbell tartan, and ice-cream by the ton from vendors spread along the esplanade. The paddle-steamers have been replaced by miniature liners, which, some say, are nothing like as steady in a high sea, but the red-and-black funnel still says MacBrayne. The Glasgow holiday crowds still pilgrimage to Staffa and Iona. In times past many of

them did so for therapeutic reasons, it being held that a good
bout of seasickness once a year toned up the system like colonic
irrigation. The crashing Atlantic rollers off Ardnamurchan Point
obliged them readily enough. The large yachts and the great grey
battleships are no more: in their place a myriad small craft fill the
bay. But when the crowds have thinned out and November gales
sweep the high seas over the shining esplanade and the winter
hibernation begins . . . I like to think that the men, women and
children who settle round the fires, and the TV, of an evening, are
not so very far removed in character, in kindness, good will and
their essential West Highland outlook from those who did the
same thing (*sans* TV) fifty years ago.